16.95'

D1486532

]

l

17

INDIAN SAHIB

Indian Sahib

QUEEN VICTORIA'S DEAR ABDUL

Sushila Anand

Duckworth

First published in 1996 by
Gerald Duckworth & Co. Ltd.
The Old Piano Factory
48 Hoxton Square, London N1 6PB
Tel: 0171 729 5986
Fax: 0171 729 0015

A catalogue record for this book is available
from the British Library

ISBN 0 7156 2718 X

Picture credits

The author and publisher are grateful to the following for supplying and giving permission to reproduce illustrations:

Jennifer Collins, pp. 22, 36, 37, 47, 55, 66, 67, 75, 79, 98
The Earl of Elgin, p. 72
English Heritage, p. 74
Majesty magazine, p. 65
National Portrait Gallery, pp. 24, 57, 95
Royal Archives, Windsor Castle, © Her Majesty Queen Elizabeth
  II, pp. 12, 13, 16, 17, 25, 28, 31, 44, 46, 59, 64, 68, 70, 71, 85, 91,
  99, 100, 103
Royal Collection Enterprises, © Her Majesty Queen Elizabeth II,
  pp. 14, 20, 38, 40, 51
Mr J. Tamplin, p. 60

Typeset by Ray Davis
Printed and bound in Great Britain by
The Bath Press, Somerset

Contents

Preface 7

Acknowledgments 10

1. Arrival 11

2. A Man of Property 23

3. Enter Rafiuddin Ahmed 35

4. Domesticity and Italian Diversions 45

5. The Fatal Christmas Card 53

6. The Munshi Triumphant 63

7. A Year of Battles 75

8. The Chill Winds of Autumn 89

9. A Prince Manqué 93

Postscript 105

Notes 107

Index 111

To the memory of my mother who
backed me up with love and devotion

Preface

I spent the year 1974/75 travelling India, and during that time came across two nineteenth-century characters whose stories had never been told. One, the Maharajah Duleep Singh, became the subject of my first biography, co-written with Michael Alexander, as we had both been working independently, each oblivious of the other's interest! The second story which impressed me was that of Abdul Karim, although my initial introduction to him was only a brief entry in Lady Lytton's Court Diary, a dusty copy of which I picked up when I was staying in Simla, the old Viceregal summer capital.

Although I realised from the outset that Abdul Karim's history had unique appeal, I held back from any attempt to write about him. One reason for my hesitancy was the scarcity of material on Abdul; as I mention in my text, very little escaped the bonfire after Queen Victoria's death, and I wondered if I could successfully conjure him up with so little to go on. However with patient searching I found certain key letters at the India Office Library, a small amount in the Royal Archives, and with that in hand began to visualise how Abdul's story might be told. It was tantalising to conjecture what *might* have been available to a biographer, had not those letters from the Queen to Abdul been committed to the flames.

When I began writing I could not have known that I would have a huge stroke of luck, as that commodity is by definition unpredictable! This good fortune happened when I was compiling a radio programme on Abdul Karim, and continued to be a blessing during the time I have been writing his story in book form. I was able to contact Michaela Reid, who had herself written the story of her husband's grandfather, Sir James

Reid, Queen Victoria's Physician. With great kindness and generosity she allowed me to look at all her family scrap books and Reid's diaries; these sources contain invaluable information which I could never have found anywhere else. I was able to get a much stronger impression of Queen Victoria's Household, and the impact made by Abdul Karim on it. It came alive, and I hope that I have been able to convey that immediacy here.

I believe that this is the first time that Munshi Abdul Karim's story has been fully told. One of the reasons for my interest is that we perceive a great deal about Queen Victoria through her reaction to Abdul; and yet though we see much, something remains mysterious. That was true also of the Queen's attachment to John Brown, the Scots ghillie, who was the utterly dependable figure she needed after Prince Albert's death more than twenty years before the advent of Abdul Karim. Victoria gradually sublimated her intense grief by making the Highlander central to her life; the enthusiasm with which she described him, the latitude in manner she allowed him, and her feelings after his death, when she described him as 'Friend more than servant', all point to a responsive woman. Moreover Queen Victoria was a person who gave both to Brown and later to the Munshi the same loyalty as she felt they gave her. Neither man was popular with the Queen's family or Household, but the unpopularity of her favourites never swayed her. Obstinate certainly, but strong in affection as well.

John Brown flourished when the Queen was a widow in her mid-forties with a young family. By the time Abdul Karim entered her life she was nearly seventy, and a very grandmotherly figure indeed. The strongest impression one gets about this old lady is her exuberance in welcoming and subsequently learning from an unknown Indian of humble birth. Given her usual sense of decorum, it was remarkable that she used her undoubted power to advance Abdul, whether or not other people thought he deserved it. Having him gazetted as the Queen's Indian Secretary would have seemed outlandish to many observers at the time.

Yet I believe that apart from her personal liking for Abdul Karim, there was something of wider significance: her interaction with him was a way of living out her belief that it was a person's character which mattered, not the outward trappings of rank. This, in the stratified society of nineteenth-century Europe, must have seemed a revolutionary idea, especially coming from the Queen, apex of the Empire.

So we are left with an impression of Queen Victoria full of curiosity, inspired by India and all things Indian, a person with strong maternal feelings in the widest sense; a woman of lively intelligence defying old age with her enjoyment of circus, music and theatre. Regal and inspiring awe, yes, but highly strung and passionate as well. In fact a very human being!

London, Spring 1996   Sushila Anand

Acknowledgments

There are many people to thank for helping to create this book:

All material from the Royal Archives is reproduced by gracious permission of Her Majesty the Queen.

Sheila de Bellaigue, Registrar, Royal Archives, Jill Kelsey, Assistant Registrar, and Frances Dimond, Curator of Photographs, Royal Archives, have been of great help in co-ordinating my research and producing relevant material.

Sir Alexander and Lady Reid have generously allowed me to use unique possessions in their family collection, and most kindly gave me hospitality in Scotland.

My thanks to the Earl of Elgin and Kincardine, who helpfully produced a photograph of the 9th Earl for me.

Staff at the India Office Library helped me unearth key letters.

Very warm thanks go to the late Colin Haycraft, who saw the possibilities in this story, and to his widow Anna as well.

My father made it possible for me to spend time completing the book.

Richard Stamp, a life-long friend, spurred me on to publication.

Two people deserve special thanks: Maurice Raynor, on whose lap-top computer I first typed the text; and Paula Sayer, of Chatland Sayer, who gave me lots of help in her own time over a long period without complaining. My debt in this respect is unrepayable.

1

Arrival

Victoria, by the Grace of God, Queen of Great Britain ....
Empress of India! The Queen had assumed the title with
alacrity, and it was with a profound sense of personal satisfaction that the proclamation was made in May 1876. For the
Queen it was no tenuous link, no abstraction, but a fitting
symbol of her concern and interest in the subcontinent that she
was destined never to see. The thought of being so distant from
it frustrated her.

In a letter to Lord Lansdowne, then Viceroy, she was to
write wistfully: 'The Queen-Empress is much interested by his
description of his tour, and is very jealous of all that he has
seen, for she would give anything to visit India!'[1]

Her age, and the long sea voyage ruled out a journey to the
fabled land, but if the Queen could not go to India, India would
come to her.

On 21st June 1887 the Queen celebrated her Golden Jubilee
and recorded vividly in her Journal:

> This very eventful day has come and is passed. All went
> off admirably ...
>
> The morning was beautiful and bright with a fresh air.
> Troops began passing early with bands playing and one
> heard constant cheering. Breakfasted with Beatrice, Ar-
> thur, Helen and Liko in the Chinese Room .... Received
> many beautiful nosegays and presents .... Then dressed,
> wearing a dress and bonnet, diamond ornaments in my
> bonnet and pearls round my neck with all my orders ....
>
> At half past 11, we left the Palace, I driving in a
> handsomely gilt landau, drawn by 6 of the creams, with
> dear Vicky and Alix who sat on the back seat. Just in front

of my carriage rode the 12 Indian officers, and in front of them my 3 sons, 5 sons-in-law, 9 grandsons and grand-sons-in-law.[2]

Abdul Karim in November 1888, showing his costume to be more that of a gentle-man than of a servant. He 'learns with extraordinary assiduity ... a thorough gentleman in feelings and manners'.

In celebration of her Jubilee the Queen had been sent a unique present, nothing less than a pair of Indian servants. Sir John Tyler, Governor of the N.W. Provinces, had been partly responsible for recruiting Indians suitable for the duties they were to perform. It was planned that the Indians should act as *khitmagars*, or table servants, in the first instance, and gradually be put to other useful tasks. So firmly did their presence take root that eventually more Indians arrived, forming a distinctive group within the Queen's ménage.

One of the first was Abdul Karim, aged twenty-four. He was

A page from the Queen's Hindustani Diary.

soon to become the Queen's friend and trusted confidant, but anathema to her Family and Household. She became his willing pupil in Hindustani and Urdu, and confided to her Journal: 'It is a great interest to me for both the language and the people, I have naturally never come into real contact with before.'[3] In her surviving exercise books we see the thick black inky outlines of the script she mastered.

In time Abdul Karim became officially the Munshi ('Teacher'); eventually he was to be gazetted the Queen's Indian Secretary, made a Companion of the Indian Empire, and decorated with the Eastern Star.

Perhaps he beguiled the old lady with a personality of refinement and grace, apparently carrying no trace of his origins in the bazaars at Agra, where his father was a *hakim*, or native doctor.

Perhaps he fed the Queen's romantic imagination with traditional stories and answered her questions about the cus-

The christening of Princess Victoria Eugenie of Battenberg in the Drawing Room at Balmoral, 23rd November 1887. Abdul Karim and another Indian servant look on. Watercolour by R.T. Pritchett.

toms, religions and aspirations of the Indian people. That these subjects held a fascination for Queen Victoria there can be no doubt. She had sent the artist Rudolph Swoboda to paint portraits of Indian people who thronged the highways and byways of the subcontinent. These now hang in the Durbar Hall at Osborne.

There is evidence in the Queen's own letters that her discussions with the Munshi were wide-ranging – philosophical, political and practical. Both head and heart were engaged. There is no doubt that the Queen found in Abdul Karim a connection with a world that was fascinatingly alien, and a confidant who would not feed her the official line. He was so far removed from the Viceroy's Court that the Queen felt she was getting much nearer to the heart, to the essence of India. She wanted to know.

Isolated by her position, and always a person to express her own views forthrightly, Queen Victoria valued those who did the same. Honesty and curiosity were her most endearing characteristics. Generosity, compassion, and a gift for friendship she had in abundance. Abdul Karim came to have a secure place in her affection, and she lavished material rewards on him and his large family – his own residence on each Royal estate, and much else besides.

Two days after the great Jubilee procession, the Queen recorded her first meeting with him:

23rd June 1887. Windsor Castle

A very fine morning with a fresh air. Felt very tired. Drove down to Frogmore with Beatrice to breakfast, and met Vicky and young Vicky there. My 2 Indian servants were there and began to wait.

The one, Mohammed Bukhsh, very dark with a very smiling expression, has been a servant before with Gen. Dennehy,[4] and also with the Rana of Dholpore, and the other, much younger, called Abdul Karim, is much lighter, tall, and with a fine serious countenance. His father is a native doctor at Agra. They both kissed my feet.[5]

Soon after Abdul's arrival, it was time for the annual trek to

Mohammed Bukhsh, who
entered the Queen's service
with Abdul Karim but re-
mained a *khitmagar*.

Balmoral, and the Queen began to exercise her mind about a
uniform for her Indian servants that would be suitable for
Scotland. She conceived the idea of tweeds cut Indian style,
and always to be worn with turban, for when the servants were
off duty. She also advised gloves, sensible shoes, and woolly
underwear for cold autumnal days. On duty, while serving
dinner, the apparel was to be white with gold turban and

trimmings. The Imperial Indians must have been imposing at all times, and most unusual when clad in their tweeds.

Even while the Queen was drawing up these instructions, Abdul Karim was moving effortlessly away from the servant class. His patron had singled him out for advancement, and it wasn't long before he abandoned more menial duties to stand at the Queen's side. As well as teaching her the Indian languages, he began to help with correspondence. Little by little, he progressed from blotting letters to discussing their content. The Queen happily watched her protégé develop his abilities. Writing to her secretary, Sir Henry Ponsonby, when sending him a Hindu vocabulary to study, and referring to a letter from Lord Dufferin, she is jubilant about the Orientals:

Sir Henry will see what he says of the Indian servants. It is just what the Queen feels and she can not say what a

Alfresco tea at Osborne, August 1887, with Abdul Karim (second from left) in his early role as *khitmagar*, along with his compatriot, Mohammed Bukhsh. Those taking tea include Princess Marie of Edinburgh, the Duke of Connaught and Princess Victoria Melita of Edinburgh (standing behind 'Grandmama') on the left, and Princess Alix and Princess Irene of Hesse on the right. A nurse holds Prince Henry of Battenberg, while his mother, Princess Henry, has her back to the camera.

comfort she finds *hers*. Abdul is most handy in helping when she *signs* by drying the signatures. He learns with extraordinary assiduity ....[6]

To Dr Reid, her Physician-in-Ordinary, with whom she was to have much communication concerning Abdul Karim in the years to come, the Queen wrote:

> I wish to observe with respect to Abdul that he has changed very much and though his manner may be grave and dignified he is very friendly and cheerful with the Queen's maids and laughs and even jokes now – and invited them to come and see all his fine things offering them fruit cake to eat ... he is very handy and intelligent and obliging and useful for his great knowledge of his own language and of course I am now quite accustomed and at home with him.[7]

On 4th April 1889 she wrote to Sir Henry again:

> As for Abdul Karim, the Queen can never praise him enough. He is zealous, attentive and quiet and gentle, has such intelligence and good sense, and (as all the Indians are) *entirely* intent on his *duty* and always ready to obey the slightest *word* or hint given. He will soon be able to *copy* a good deal for the Queen – even in French – and is an excellent accountant. He is a *thorough* gentleman in feelings and manners.[8]

As fast as Abdul rose in the Queen's estimation, he attracted scorn and contempt from her Household with equal speed. In an age when no Englishman of rank would easily mix socially with any Indian other than a Prince, the ladies and gentlemen at Court found it insufferable that they should be made to do so. Any association with him, which the Queen urged, was despised.

Abdul, for his part, was growing into the role of favourite very comfortably.

On the evening of 26th April 1889, the Prince of Wales was host at Sandringham for a command performance, in which Henry Irving and Ellen Terry were to perform. Their pièce de resistance was to be *The Bells*, following the huge success of this melodrama at the Lyceum Theatre in London. Irving's legendary performance was perhaps enough to justify the choice.

Much effort went into recreating the stage setting and effects which had made such a powerful impression on London audiences, including the very sleigh in which the villain flees when he fancies that he hears the bells! Rounding off the evening on a more tranquil note Ellen Terry was to appear as Portia, no doubt delivering 'the quality of mercy' speech in classic style. Three hundred guests, including royalty, friends with estates nearby, and tenants assembled in the ballroom, which for this occasion had become the Theatre Royal. According to the *Morning Post* of 27th April, it was 'a spacious and handsome apartment which faces the avenue of limes by which the east front of Sandringham House is reached.'[9]

The Queen, who had arrived two days earlier, included the Munshi in her suite. As the guests took their seats, the Munshi found that he had only been allocated a place with the servants. Feeling his dignity thereby deeply affronted, he stalked out and retired moodily to his room. When the Queen came to hear of it, she backed him up, saying that indeed Abdul should always sit with the Household.

It was noted that in the autumn of that year, at the Braemar Games, the Munshi took his place beside the gentry.

Naturally the growing animosity shown by members of the Household towards Abdul Karim did not go unnoticed by Queen Victoria. During the last twenty years of her life, she relied heavily on her personal physician, Dr (later Sir) James Reid, not only for his professional ministrations, but as general adviser in matters relating to the Munshi. The latter was not a role he enjoyed. In the years to come he would find it a great strain, as the Queen used him as both lightning conductor and confessor when conflict surrounding Abdul Karim was at its height.

Reid himself, an Aberdonian Scot, was a man of equable temper, well liked by other members of the Royal Household, and his diaries reveal much about the relationship between Monarch and Munshi. An incident in June 1889 was to prove a portent.

After taking tea with Abdul in the cottage at Balmoral, the

Queen apparently found one of her favourite brooches missing on the return drive. It was normally used to fasten the Queen's shawl, and her dresser Mrs Tuck had attached it thereon. The Queen was much upset. Rankin, a footman on duty that day, suspected Abdul Karim's brother-in-law, one Hourmet Ali, of having taken it. The brooch eventually turned up at Wagland's, a jeweller in Windsor. When Mr Wagland confirmed that an Indian had sold it to him for six shillings, the Munshi's enemies were exultant. The brooch was retrieved and taken back to the Queen, who was 'much surprised' at its reappearance.

However, when Mrs Tuck, the unfortunate dresser, ventured to report Hourmet's involvement, the Queen became very angry indeed, shouting 'That's what you British call justice.'[10]

This incident was the first indication that the Queen would always choose to defend Abdul Karim – that she was deaf to

The Garden Cottage at Balmoral, where the Queen enjoyed working, attended by Abdul Karim. Watercolour by William Simpson.

criticism of him. Her defence was to grow more dogged as the forces combined against the Munshi became more resolute.

As if to underline her growing pleasure in his company, in the autumn she made a surprising decision, and we have a note from Dr Reid to his predecessor, Sir William Jenner, giving the news:

> 17th October 1889
>
> The Queen is off today to Glassalt Shiel to stay there till tomorrow. She has not done this since 1882, having given it up when Brown died, and said she would never sleep there again. However she has changed her mind and has taken Abdul with her![11]

Glassalt Shiel was the Queen's very private retreat on Loch Muick, where she could spend time in rustic simplicity. It calmed her nerves. As for her choice of companion – Abdul was one of the small party that accompanied her – where others saw only an ambitious upstart the Queen saw a man of charm and gentleness.

It is not unlikely that, despite his humble beginnings, Abdul Karim had about him the courtliness of Islamic tradition. Did he include popular quotations from Urdu poets in the lessons for his Royal pupil? He would probably have been familiar enough with the genre to convey the subtle romantic ardour with which it is suffused. If so, the septuagenarian Queen may well have been completely won over, particularly if 'dear good Abdul' spoke those verses as if to her. Within that dumpy black bombazined figure there was a spirit which always responded to the chivalrous male.

Equally, the Queen had a gift for mothering some unlikely people, as witness her behaviour towards the errant Maharajah Duleep Singh, much earlier in her reign, after whose death she continued her material support of his numerous children. However, the Maharajah was himself Royal, and the Queen's inclination to care about an outsider like Abdul Karim is more startling.

In February 1890, while at Windsor, the by now indispensable Abdul became ill, suffering from a painful carbuncle on his neck. The Queen solicited Dr Reid's assurance, as she was 'much troubled' by the Munshi's distress. She was 'always very anxious about them all, lest the climate should not agree with them'.[12]

On 1st March Reid confided to his diary:

Queen visiting Abdul twice daily, in his room taking Hindustani lessons, signing her boxes, examining his neck, smoothing his pillows, etc.[13]

Dr James Reid, Personal Physician to the Queen, in 1884. He was made a baronet in 1897.

2

A Man of Property

Three years after his arrival at Windsor, Abdul Karim had sufficiently ingratiated himself with the Queen that she wished to bestow on him a signal mark of recognition. Whether a grant of land was her own idea or one inspired by the Munshi is not known, but whichever it was the Queen pursued the project vigorously. Always an avid correspondent with her Viceroys, she began by writing to Lord Lansdowne.

July 11th 1890

The Queen-Empress telegraphed to the Viceroy last Friday 4th, as she had not had time to write, which she does today. She writes first to say that she is delighted with his daughter, who resembles both her parents, and who is so particularly quiet and ladylike ….

The other subject she cyphered as having much at heart was what Lord Cross wrote to him about, viz with respect to a grant of land to her really exemplary and excellent young Munshi, Hafiz Abdul Karim, who is quite a confidential servant, – (she does not mean in a literal sense, for he is not a servant) – and most useful to her with papers, letters, books, etc.

It is the first time in the world that any Native has ever held such a position, and she is very anxious to mark this permanently – the more so, as the wish to do anything for his good and respectable father, Dr Wuzeeredin [sic], failed on account of his age, and smaller and really very unimportant promotions to others of his family, which the Queen knows have over and over again been given to people with less merit by officials who were interested in them, were refused. This being the case, the Queen hopes, whenever it is most feasible, that this will be done as a mark of approbation of the Queen Empress. The Queen always rewards and promotes those who have served, or do serve her well in England, and has generally found those whom she asked to assist her in this ready to do so. When the Viceroy goes to Agra, the Queen Empress hopes he will see Dr Wuzeeredin, and tell him how satisfied she is with his son ....[1]

The 5th Marquess of Lansdowne, K.G., Viceroy of India 1888-1893, with some of the 'heaven-born' in the grounds of Viceregal Lodge, Simla, in 1890. Front, left to right: Sir Philip Percival Hutchins; the Rt. Hon. Sir Andrew Scoble; Frederick Sleigh Roberts; Lord Lansdowne; Sir George Chesney; Sir Charles Elliott; Sir David Miller Barbour. Back, left to right: Sir Edward Buck; Sir Anthony Macdonnell; Mr Harvey James; William de la Poer, Lord Beresford (Secretary to the Viceroy); Col. George Brazier-Creagh; Maj.-Gen. Sir John Ardagh; Lt.-Gen. Sir Edwin Hayter; Maj.-Gen. Sir Wykeham Pemberton; Mr Jenkinson.

Theatricals to while away
the Christmas holidays at
Osborne, January 1888:
'Solomon and Sheba', with
Sir Henry Ponsonby as
Solomon and Princess
Beatrice as the Queen of
Sheba, attended by Abdul
Karim (top left) and
Mohammed Bukhsh.

Having once set the ball rolling, the Queen was anxious that
the matter should advance quickly. On 1st August a telegram
was wired, the first of many to be exchanged on this subject:

1st August 1890. 3.50 pm (Received 2nd. 6.30 am)
To: Viceroy, Simla.

Letter 5th July received 13th. Wish you to proceed with
grant of land for Munshi. That that might not be less than
five to six hundred rupees. Position peculiar and without
precedent. Father was only transferred, not promoted.
Brother's place not much promotion either. My last letter
explains.[2]

The wires had been humming.

Telegram 1st August 1890
From the Viceroy to the Queen Empress.

The Viceroy has now given instructions to the proper
officials, and he hopes to be able to report the result to
your Majesty very shortly. He has said that the grant of
land should, if possible, be not far from Agra, but he has
yet to learn whether any land is available in that neigh-
bourhood …. There is in these days very great difficulty
in obtaining land suitable for such a purpose.[3]

Reconnaissance of suitable land was no doubt proceeding,
but not fast enough for the Queen's liking! On 28th August
Landsowne received a further telegram at Viceregal Lodge,
Simla, pressing that the land to be granted to Abdul Karim
should definitely yield more than six hundred rupees yearly 'as
that so little'.[4]

Having fired this salvo, the Queen no doubt settled back to
enjoy the pleasures of Osborne, her favourite home. Nothing
further was heard of the matter for some weeks, whether from
reluctance to comply with the Queen's wishes, genuine difficulty in finding suitable land to grant in such peculiar circumstances, or simply the delays of bureaucracy. A letter from the
Viceroy finally arrived in the autumn, but it was inconclusive,
and we find that by October the Queen was growing impatient
again, particularly as Abdul was going on leave.

Balmoral Castle October 16th 1890
To the Viceroy, Lord Lansdowne

The Queen-Empress thanks the Viceroy very much for
his kind letter of 23rd September. She is a little disappointed that the grant of land for her excellent Munshi
Abdul Karim has not yet been accomplished, as she would
like this to have been the case before he left for India on
leave on 30th. However he is quite content to wait till it
can be settled, and he will be the bearer of a letter from
the Queen-Empress to the Viceroy, whom he hopes to pay
his respects to at Agra. The Queen is very glad that he is
going out on the same ship as Lady Lansdowne, and she

trusts that the gales which we have had many of lately will have subsided by that time.[5]

Whether Lady Lansdowne was pleased to have the Munshi on the same ship is not recorded.

However, Abdul did not go empty-handed when he took leave of the Queen-Empress, a parting which affected her, as the following letter shows. Whether she had completely given up thoughts of ever embarking for India herself, the Queen must have projected her presence on that voyage in her imagination.

Balmoral Castle October 29th 1890

The Queen gives these few lines to be delivered to the Viceroy by her excellent and much esteemed Munshi and Indian Clerk, Hafiz Abdul Karim, whom she recommends to the Viceroy's special notice.

His absence for four months will be severely felt by her, as he is very useful and helpful in so many ways. The Queen-Empress trusts that the gift of land may soon be effected, for it is four months since it was first spoken of. The Munshi's father, Dr Wuzeeridin [*sic*], is, the Queen believes, about to retire after 32 or 33 years' good service, and she hopes he will have a good pension. The Queen would be glad if his son-in-law, also a Doctor, Ilam Ullah, who has 25 years service, and is a doctor in Agra Jail, could succeed in Dr Wuzeeridin's place if feasible. The Queen-Empress trusts that the Viceroy has entirely recovered from his attacks of fever.[6]

We have a glimpse of the Queen's life at this period, graciously doing her duty, while Abdul was preparing for his voyage. Mr Scheffer, the Queen of Roumania's private secretary, who had accompanied her to Balmoral in October 1890, gave the *Figaro* an account of his stay there. The report is headed 'THE QUEEN AS HOSTESS, Her Majesty's Dinner Party', and the text begins by asserting that in giving his impressions of Balmoral Mr Scheffer has given a beautiful picture of the Queen's life in her favourite Highland residence. It continues with a a description of the reception at Ballater, where the special train stopped:

Here is the Prince of Wales, looking perhaps too much of a good fellow in his kilted costume, de rigueur for the Royal Princes in Scotland. He is the first to smile at his unusual appearance. Prince Henry of Battenberg is very martial and good looking in the same uniform, and beside him gentle and weakly, the young Duke of Clarence. Two ladies, simple in dress and manner, come up to kiss the Queen. They are Princess Beatrice and the Duchess of

Balmoral Castle, photographed from near the Garden Cottage.

Albany. We drive in open carriages. Scattered in the pine woods the white cottages of Ballater seem to smile upon us. The road passes between meadows and hills. The air is chilly and faint with the scent of heather, of pine, and of mown grass. An autumn mist bounds the horizon, tinges the landscape with blue, gives a charming dreaminess to the outlines of the hills. It is a long drive in the wide and lonely valley, where the river, according to the fall of the sun's rays, glides silvery or like ebony on a level with its green banks. Suddenly beyond a lawn the white castle appears, surrounded by foot hills backed with bare and ruddy summits. It is not an imposing structure notwithstanding the turrets on its pacific walls, and it does not give the idea of a Royal residence. But it is unique and unexpected in this site of heath and mountain –. No guards, police, or soldiers. ...

A Highland dance was given in honour of the Queen of Roumania. The writer was looking on, when suddenly he felt the attraction of a human presence behind him, and in spite of himself he turned back.

Leaning on a tall stick, a gentle face under white hair, dressed in mourning – it was Queen Victoria, who attended the war-like pantomime unexpected, still and silent. She looked like a fairy of the awe-inspiring sort, so different from her portraits, from the sad countenance she has in public. She advanced towards the door with a wonderfully elastic step, and as she spoke to me, her clear eye fixed upon me, I had the feeling that, short in stature as she was, I was dwarfed by her presence. The Queen wore at dinner the splendid diamonds given by the city of Bombay. She sat still and silent at the upper end of the table, with her Indian servants behind her like a picture of the early Italian religious painters. The guests, however, spoke to each other without the least restraint. My neighbour at table, the Princess Beatrice, hummed a tune played on the chapel organ and asked me whether I knew it. The Queen of Roumania spoke with her usual ardour. Private conversation soon became general. The Duke of Clarence in an undertone makes some remarks to his young sister, very girlishly beautiful in pink and white, and who, keeping very stiffly in her chair, is choking with her effort to suppress her laughter. ... The dining room is of almost puritan simplicity. The dinner service is plain but in perfect taste. The Sovereign casts a quiet and kindly look over the table where humble guests sit beside Royalties without any regard to etiquette. On her bare shoulders the gems flash more brightly beside the lace and black silk. The decanters of cut glass sparkle with rare wines, gold and red only. One glass is set before the Queen, and the Hindoo, having filled it three-quarters full with water, adds the traditional whisky. The room where we adjourn after dinner is hung with Scotch hangings, rather crude to our eyes accustomed to more subdued tones. ...

During the conversation with which I was honoured by Her Majesty, I again felt this curious sensation of being subdued by that little woman who, leaning with both hands on her stick, looked up to me. The Queen of Roumania ... rose to read one of her poems. Queen Victoria was in the full light, her very white hair appearing under her widow's cap, and she listened, very attentive and serious. A little further off, her face slightly turned aside, her neck imprisoned with pearls, her white hands, covered with rings, resting on her red dress, sat the Princess of Wales with her puzzling and persistent smile. Still further off in the shadow were Princess Beatrice, with her strongly aquiline nose; the Duchess of Albany, with the profile of a bird; Prince Henry of Battenberg, anxious for everybody's comfort; the Cabinet Minister in attendance, and eight or ten invited guests of the suite. The Queen listened as Carmen Sylva [the Queen of Roumania] was reading, and seemed affected by her rich, sweet voice.

Early in the morning the visitors took leave of Queen Victoria in the private apartments. The Queen of Roumania got into one of the carriages outside, and bowed and smiled, as a servant covered her with plaids and furs, when suddenly and altogether unexpectedly the black fairy with white hair, Queen Victoria, appeared. A little trembling, and her eyes filled with tears, she hastened to the carriage, and a last time with motherly kindness embraced the exquisite Sovereign who had won her heart.[7]

Scenes from 'Rebecca', a tableau vivant performed at Balmoral in October 1888, with Miss Minnie Cochrane (above centre) in the title part and Abdul Karim as Eleazer. The cast also included Miss Moore (above left), Mrs Campbell (above right), Ahmed Hussain (above, far left) and Mohammed Bukhsh (below right).

Abdul Karim duly arrived in India. The Queen's missive, carried and delivered in person by him on 23rd November brought a swift response from the Viceroy. He was able to tell the Queen that Karim had been granted an audience. The Queen's response was equally speedy.

Telegram: 24th November 1890. 7.35 pm

Accept warm thanks from me and Munshi for great kindness today.[8]

A letter from the Viceroy dated 6th November had just reached the Queen; it announced the completion of Karim's land grant. This was 'highly satisfactory to her in every way', and she 'again owes warm thanks to the Viceroy'.[9]

Once the Munshi had arrived, he posed a delicate diplomatic problem: just what was his status? How should he be treated? His only claim to the Viceroy's attention was the Queen's wish that he should be received with some dignity, as befitted a figure in whom she took a special interest. Abdul Karim did not fit neatly into the hierarchy, so finely judged. Lord Lansdowne wrote a less than reassuring letter to the Queen:

Agra, November 26th 1890

The Viceroy presents his humble duty to the Queen-Empress, and begs to say that he has had the honour of receiving your Majesty's letter of October 29th, which was handed to him by Abdul Karim on 23rd instant. Sir John Tyler, at the Viceroy's invitation, brought Abdul Karim to see him on the morning after his arrival, and the Munshi subsequently had an interview with Lady Lansdowne.

Abdul Karim's position as Munshi does not give him a right to be included amongst the regular 'Durbaris'. All officials below a certain rank are excluded from these, and the admission of any person of lower standing would be much resented by the rest. As however, Abdul Karim holds an appointment in your Majesty's Household, it seemed only natural and proper that he should, upon such an occasion, attend upon your Majesty's representative with the members of his staff.

Sir John Tyler dealt with the grant of land which has

been made to Abdul Karim, and spoke in Abdul Karim's presence with, what seemed to the Viceroy, a very unbecoming indifference to the signal recompense which the Munshi has received.

In regard to this matter the Viceroy thinks it his duty to tell your Majesty that a grant, such as that which has been made to Abdul Karim, is most rarely bestowed in this country, and then only to officers of very long and meritorious service. As an illustration he may mention that quite recently one of the men who at the peril of his life, and under a withering fire helped to blow up the Kashmir Gate of Delhi in the Mutiny, received, on retirement from the service, a grant of land yielding only Rs 250 for life.

Abdul Karim, at the age of 26 has received a perpetual grant of land representing an income of more than double that amount in recognition of his services as a member of your Majesty's Household.

The Viceroy does not, for a moment, question that service rendered to the Queen Empress should receive special and signal recognition, but he must protest against such rewards, when they have been given at your Majesty's express desire, being underrated, or spoken of as though they were not of serious importance.[10]

The Queen was alarmed that this contretemps might have prejudiced opinion against Abdul Karim:

She could not help being a good deal annoyed, as her wish was that her good Munshi should make the favourable impression which he deserves from his character, education, and excellence, and she was so afraid this might have done him harm in the Viceroy's eyes. He himself is deeply grateful to Lord and Lady Lansdowne …[11]

Despite this unpromising interlude, the most important thing had been accomplished to the Queen's satisfaction. Abdul Karim's position had been secured.

3

Enter Rafiuddin Ahmed

In December 1892, the respected *Strand Magazine* had obtained a Royal scoop: the author, a certain Rafiuddin Ahmed, was able to reproduce a page from Queen Victoria's Diary written in Hindustani, accompanied by a portrait of the Queen, allegedly given to the author, who was described as 'an eminent Indian scholar'. The editorial heading informed readers that 'Her Majesty was good enough to copy the two pages from her Diary expressly for this article.'[1]

Who exactly was Rafiuddin Ahmed? Certain facts about him can be established, but ultimately he remains a chameleon-like figure.

Born in 1865, he was educated at the Deccan College, Poona. Then like many young Indians towards the end of the nineteenth century, he turned up in London as a student, first at King's College, London. Subsequently a member of the Middle Temple, he was called to the Bar in 1892, but like many of his generation he also had political ambitions. These he expressed as a member of the Muslim League, of which he appears to have been a co-founder. It was claimed that he was also a supporter of doubtful, possibly insurgent elements, which were then beginning to coalesce against British Rule in India.

Perhaps Rafiuddin hoped to emulate Dadabhai Nairoji, the first Indian to take his seat in the House of Commons. Rafiuddin had himself tried unsuccessfully to stand for Parliament, but had made a name for himself as contributor to the *Pall Mall Gazette* and *Black and White*, as well as to the *Strand Magazine*.

At some point his path had crossed the Munshi's – a friendship he had fostered, according to his detractors, for his own ends. Police intelligence had marked him as a troublemaker in

'The British Empire', celebrated in its heyday at the Court of Queen Victoria in 1892.

India; and with this reputation his appearance in Britain had been noted by the authorities. Suspicion was rife that Mr Ahmed was an agent of the Amir of Afghanistan. As such, his proximity to Abdul Karim, and through him it seemed to the Queen herself, was naturally viewed with alarm. Ahmed may only have been the most minor of players in the Great Game, but he was nonetheless subject to investigation by Sir Ernest Bradford, Chief of the Metropolitan Police. Surveillance was also carried out on the Munshi.

Rafiuddin had obviously used his connection with Abdul Karim to procure a rare specimen of the Queen's Diary, publication of which allowed him to bask in a little reflected glory.

His extraordinary style can be sampled in the following paragraphs from the *Strand Magazine*:

VIII.
"Marche Indienne, from L'Africaine" *(Meyerbeer)*.

TABLEAU:

"EMPIRE."

H.R.H. Princess Christian of Schleswig Holstein.
H.R.H. Princess Beatrice (Princess Henry of Battenberg).
The Hon. Evelyn Paget.   The Hon. Mary Hughes.
Miss McNeill.   Miss Minnie Cochrane.   Miss de Horsey.
The Marquis of Lorne.   Mr. Muther.
Mr. Arthur Ponsonby.   Mr. Henry Cowell.
The Munsi Hafiz Abdul Karim.   Mirza Yusuf Beg.
Ahmad Khan. Gholam Mustafa. Khuda Bakhsh. Damuda.
Incidental Music, "Rule Britannia."

GOD SAVE THE QUEEN.

The Music by the Band of the Royal Marine Light Infantry,
GEORGE MILLER, Bandmaster.

Costumier, Mr. NATHAN. ♦ Perruquier, Mr. CLARKSON.
The Scenery by Mr. COLE.
Stage Manager, The Hon. ALEXANDER YORKE.

Queen Victoria is admired and adored by millions besides
her own subjects, not so much because she is the Sovereign of Great Britain (though that in itself is a unique
distinction) but because she unites in herself political,
moral and intellectual qualities of the highest order,
granted by Providence only to the chosen few …. But the
quality which would endear her most to posterity is her
intellectual eminence …. Nothing surprises us more than
her wide information, her sweet and modest expression,
and her logical and learned remarks in the course of
conversation. But the latest display of her mental activity,
which eclipses all past achievements in her literary pur-
suits, will come as an agreeable surprise upon all lovers
of learning in every part of the world.

Her Majesty the Queen, with all the duties and respon-
sibilities incident to the possession of the Imperial scep-
tre, finds time to learn an oriental language, and has

The enigmatic Rafiuddin Ahmed, barrister, journalist and possibly secret agent, painted by Rudolph Swoboda at the Queen's request in 1893.

actually made so great a progress the last three years as to be able to write a separate diary in the Hindustani language.

It is interesting to hear that Mr Gladstone can deliver lectures, write articles and review novels at his age, it is much more so to know that his Sovereign Lady, at her age, can master a new language entirely alien to the people of Europe, acquaint herself with the philosophy of the East, read the sentiments of her Eastern subjects in the vernacular, and keep a daily account of her work in her new language. It is all the more interesting because the Queen does it with a sincere desire to know the wants, manners, and customs, ways and thoughts of the people, and particularly the women, of India. The rapidity and ease with which the Queen is mastering the language is very remarkable. Among her many enviable qualities, there are two which the Queen possesses in an eminent degree. These are strict regularity and firm determination …. I may say no pressure of work, no anxiety, no sorrow keeps her from her linguistic work. Every day at the appointed hour the Queen is busy with her Hindustani. Even during the hours of most poignant pain and bewildering grief, enough to upset the daily routine of ordinary minds, the Queen did not fail to write her Hindustani Diary at the usual time. For the first time in the history of Europe a Sovereign of a Great Power has devoted herself seriously to the literature of the Orient.[2]

Naturally no account of the Royal Scholar would have been complete without mention of her teacher, who is given credit for 'his assiduous and responsible services'.[3]

The article suggests that Ahmed had been honoured by conversations with the Turkish Sultan in Constantinople, and was a probable emissary from the Queen to any number of Eastern potentates.

The reality of a fully-fledged diplomatic career eluded him, though the Queen did her utmost to recommend him to Lord Salisbury, urgently asking him to grant Ahmed an interview, to see whether a place might not be found where he could use the diplomatic skills she believed him to possess. It is more than likely that, even if Ahmed had lacked the opportunity to forward his ambition face to face with the Queen, his friend Abdul Karim had done so thoroughly by proxy. Or had Rafiuddin been able to confide in the Queen during those conversations when he'd noted her sweetness and modesty of expression?

His deftly placed hints about tête-à-tête encounters with the Queen gain some credence when we find him invited to the Duke of York's[4] wedding on 6th July 1893. A further mark of the Queen's approval lay in her arranging for him to sit for Swoboda – very successfully as it turned out. The artist used a

The wedding of George, Duke of York, and Princess Mary of Teck, 6th July 1893, in the Chapel Royal, St James's Palace. Painting by Laurits R. Tuxen.

subtle palette of dusty pink and bottle green for Ahmed's costume; his portrayal of the face may have been a touch flattering.

The Queen certainly had a notion, which she put forward confidently, as to the benefit of sending a Moslem with Ahmed's cultural background as emissary to the Turkish Sultan, and she pursued this steadily over the next few years. No less a person than Dr Jowett, Master of Balliol College, Oxford, also encouraged Rafiuddin in his ambitions.

In fact Rafiuddin's services were utilised twice unofficially in the early nineties during the difficulties with Turkey, when he went to Constantinople with letters of introduction from the Foreign Office and had interviews with Sultan Abdul Hamid. It was the Queen's mark of appreciation for this mission that prompted her to recommend his appointment to the British embassy there.

A memorandum from the office of Charles A. Bayley, of the Thuggee and Dacoity Department in India, expresses somewhat less confidence than the Queen had apparently invested in Mr Ahmed.

> In April last, Sir A. Martin informed Mr Clarke, Assistant Secretary in the Foreign Dept, that Sardar Nasrulla Khan, when in England made an arrangement with Mr Rafiu-d-din of Gray's Inn, studying as a barrister, to forward information to Ghulam Miyyu-d-din of Bulbul Bazaar, Calcutta, who is general recipient in India of information for the Amir ...
>
> Some of the most extraordinary stories thus find their way from English palaces to the Kabul Court, and the dish, always more or less spicey, is obviously prepared to suit the assumed taste of the recipient. Hatred of everything English inspires the writer of these productions, who is well known to the Secret Police as a gentleman who is believed to make a good thing of trading on his friendship with the Queen's Munshi.[5]

The Munshi and Rafiuddin may have been adroit at teaming up for their mutual benefit, but this opportunism could not have given them the success they enjoyed at Court had it not been for the Queen's generosity of outlook and wide sympathy. Considering the Queen's attitude to all 'her Indians', there seems no doubt that she was remarkably free from prejudice and much more alert to it than was usual during her lifetime.

4

Domesticity and Italian Diversions

In less than five years the Munshi had risen from very humble origins to be a 'pukka sahib'. The Queen had decorated him with the Order of the Eastern Star and had generously seen to his material needs. We catch a glimpse of his domestic arrangements in the descriptions written by those who paid him a visit, which seems to have included almost anyone of note who came to Court. Not everyone presented him with gifts as lavish as the Tsar's, who on one occasion gave a gold and enamel tea service, but that was by no means an isolated incidence of largesse.

In the winter of 1890/91, newly enriched with property, Abdul Karim had embarked alone for England. Two years later his wife accompanied him. She was naturally the object of much curiosity, and was greeted first by Queen Victoria:

November 18th 1893

A blowy disagreeable day, – Abdul has just returned from 6 months leave, and brought his wife back with him from India. She and her mother are staying at the Frogmore Cottage, which I had arranged for them, and I went down with Ina McNeill to see them. The Munshi's wife wore a beautiful sari of crimson gauze. She is nice looking, but would not raise her eyes, she was so shy.[1]

Soon the Queen was visiting the Frogmore Cottage regularly. One can hardly imagine what impression the shy wife formed of the Queen-Empress, whom she would have known hitherto only as a figure carved in granite or marble, meant to adorn some public area in a dusty Indian town. Now she found

The Munshi Hafiz Abdul
Karim, November 1892.

herself not only in the land of the white sahibs, 'the heaven-
born', but befriended by the Queen, who had a semi-divine
status in the eyes of her Indian subjects. No wonder she could
hardly raise her eyes.

The object of this reverence found plenty to say about the

fact that the Munshi's wife and household were dwelling nearby, and she confided Abdul's happiness in having them in a letter to her eldest daughter, the Empress Frederick of Germany:

December 9th 1893. Windsor Castle

... I don't think I told you of the two Indian ladies who are here now, and who are, I believe, the first Mohammedan purdah ladies who ever came over ... and keep their custom of complete seclusion and of being entirely covered when they go out, except for holes for their eyes. They are the wife of my Munshi ... and her Mother. The former is pretty with beautiful eyes ... she was beautifully dressed with green and red and blue gauzes spangled with gold, very gracefully draped over head and body ....

The Queen was obviously surprised to find the mother not wearing a sari, but instead tight-fitting silk trousers, with overblouse and shawl, a typical North Indian style which the Queen thought 'looks like a man'. She acknowledges that they were 'shy and frightened the first, but not the second time'.[3]

Within a month the Queen had become sufficiently au fait with the Munshi's ménage to know that the couple were having difficulties in their attempt to have a baby. Concern about the situation led her to intervene by asking Dr Reid's advice, and after consulting him she wrote the following letter:

Windsor Castle. 12th December 1893

My dear Abdul

I spoke to Dr Reid about your dear Wife and I think he will understand easily what you have to tell him. It may be that in hurting her foot and leg she may have twisted (moved or hurt) something in her inside, which would account for things not being regular and as they ought.

If this is so, it can only be found out by her being examined (felt) by the hand of this Lady Doctor. Many, many 1000 ladies have to go through this with a Doctor, which is very disagreeable – but with a Lady Dr there can be no objection, and without that you can not find out what is the matter.

Sheikh Chidda in atten-
dance on Queen Victoria as
she works in the grounds
of Frogmore House, July
1893.

It may be something is out of its place which can be put
right and then the object of your great wishes may be
obtained. There is nothing I would not do to help you both,
as you are my dear Indian Children and you can say
anything to me. I have had 9 children myself and have
had daughters, daughters-in-law, nieces, grandchildren
etc. to look after and I can help you.
    Your loving Mother
    Victoria R.I.[4]

A Maid of Honour wrote a more detailed account of the
Munshi's wife, this time at Balmoral:

I have just been to see the Munshi's wife (by Royal Command). She is fat. Not uncomely, a delicate shade of chocolate and gorgeously attired, rings on her fingers, rings on her nose, a pocket mirror set in Turquoises on her thumb and every feasible part of her person hung with charms and bracelets and earrings, a rose pink veil on her head bordered with heavy gold and splendid silver and satin swathing round her person. She speaks English in a limited manner and declares she likes the cold. The house surrounded by a twenty foot palisade, the door opening of

Osborne, summer 1894. Among those present in this group of members of the Queen's Household are Lady Churchill (seated, left) and the Hon. Alexander Yorke, Master of Ceremonies for Royal Theatricals (seated on the floor, centre). Behind, from the left, are Sir Henry Ponsonby, Private Secretary to the Queen, Sir Arthur Bigge, Assistant Private Secretary, and Dr Reid. Sir John Cowell stands at the far right.

itself, the white figure emerging silently from a near
chamber, all seemed so un-English, so essentially oriental, that we could hardly believe that we were within a
hundred yards of the castle.[2]

Friendly calls by the Queen and her daughters became
usual, wherever the Court was in residence.

Osborne, Dec. 28/93

Would you and your wife prefer if I only brought Beatrice, or might Victoria who is so interested in India come
at the same time or would she rather only see one at a
time? Perhaps tomorrow morning would do?
Your affte friend, V.R.I.[5]

In February 1894, the Queen travelled to Florence for her
Spring holiday, where she was to stay at the magnificent Villa
Fabbricotti, which had once housed Bonaparte's sister,
Pauline Borghese. The first floor rooms which she was to
occupy had windows which gave onto a terrace, commanding a
view of the entire city and the landscape beyond. Also allocated
rooms at the same level were the Munshi, with Prince and
Princess Henry of Battenberg, Lady Churchill, the Hon. Harriet Phipps, and Dr Reid.

The *Standard* informed its readers, in a preview of the
Queen's visit: 'The villa is among the most ancient of the many
luxurious residences built for their own occupation by wealthy
Florentines – it has 56 rooms,'[6] while *Truth* divulged that the
Oriental attendants were to be lodged in a detached tower in
the grounds, 'where they will be able to enjoy complete seclusion when so disposed'.[7]

The Munshi was no longer included among the 'Oriental
attendants'. The idyllic calm of a Florentine spring, intended
to give the Queen a much-needed boost to her health and
well-being, was interrupted by discontent amongst her Household. Seemingly intent on stirring up trouble for the Munshi,
someone in the tightly-knit circle surrounding the Queen had
made enquiries about his origins.

From India had come news that Abdul Karim was of a
humble family; surely no surprise. Perhaps the only minor

revelation had been that his father was no prestigious army doctor, as Karim had asserted, but a *hakim* (traditional healer), untrained in Western medicine: He seems to have been a Hospital Assistant, earning around 60 Rupees a month.

Evidently gossip was rife, probably as a result of the original letter being given press publicity. Suddenly, this Spring it seemed that the Munshi's background and position were on the agenda. There was growing controversy, and mixed up in it was none other than Rafiuddin Ahmed.

A letter addressed to the Editor of the *Westminster Gazette* from a certain Gore Ouseley of Notting Hill, published on 6th April 1894, comes straight to the point:

The Queen's Munshi
To the Editor of the Westminster Gazette

Sir, – Mr Rafiuddin Ahmed endeavours to show the cause why a native of India of the lower middle-class should be treated on an equality with the nobility of England. The Queen has an undoubted right to favour whom she likes, but is it not going too far when she expects her guests to associate with a man who is greatly their inferior, in rank at any rate? Perhaps Mr Rafiuddin Ahmed imagines that the unsophisticated and gullible Radical believes a Munshi to be a prince or something of that sort in 'them foreign parts', but he knows, and I know, the intrinsic value of one in India. Mr Ahmad [*sic*] is perfectly aware of the fact that if his countryman was at this moment in his native city of Lahore he would most probably be sitting on a high stool in a Government office, copying letters, or engaged in some such commendable but scarcely princely task on a stipend of 50s or 100s per mensem at the outside, and that if he ever had the good fortune to attend a Lieutenant-Governor's levee – leaving out of the question any Viceregal affair – his only means of doing so would be to enlist himself as a table servant.

I wonder what the Hyderabad nobles would say if the Nizam were to import a Board School assistant – whose position is far above a Munshi's – and expect them to play Tom, Dick and Harry with him. And the Nizam's is only a petty State. I am, Sir, your obedient servant.

Gore Ouseley   Notting Hill, April 5[8]

It was to the original correspondence, which had started all
the fuss, that the Queen referred in a letter to her Secretary,
Henry Ponsonby, memorable for its irate tone as she defended
Abdul:

> Florence, April 10th 1894
>
> The Queen wrote rather in a hurry when she mentioned
> to him the stupid ill natured Article or rather letter about
> the poor good Munshi and she wd. wish to observe that to
> make out that he is *low* is really *outrageous* and in a
> country like England quite out of place – She has known
> 2 Archbishops who were the sons respectively of a
> Butcher and a Grocer, a Chancellor (Campbell) whose
> father was a poor sort of Scotch Minister, Sir D. Stewart
> and Ld Mt Stephen both who ran about barefoot as chil-
> dren and whose parents were very humble, and the
> Tradesmen Maple and J. Price were made Baronets! Ab-
> dul's father saw good and honourable service as a Dr. and
> he (Abdul) feels cut to the heart at being thus spoken of.
> It probably comes from some low jealous Indians or
> Anglo-Indians and N …. The Queen is so sorry for the poor
> Munshi's sensitive feelings.[9]

To add insult to injury in the Queen's eyes, Dr Reid, whom
she regarded as one of the less prejudiced members of her staff,
was cataloguing the Munshi's alleged misdemeanours on the
journey to Florence.

These included 'complaint to the Queen about the position
of his carriage onwards from Bologna'; not allowing the
Queen's maids access to the bathroom; his wife and mother-in-
law 'performing functions' in their saloon; and lastly the con-
ceit which had led Abdul Karim to select several photographs
of the Queen, to be displayed in a local shop window to mark
her Florentine visit – grouped round a large portrait of himself![10]

Reid obviously could not forgive this vanity. When the Munshi composed a brief autobiography, to be published in the
Florence Gazette, along with a flattering photo, the messenger
entrusted with it complained to the Queen.

She must have been amused. Certainly it would appear that

Von Angeli's perceptive
study of Abdul Karim.

she had more sense of proportion than her Household. Did she
have a wicked sense of humour too? Why else did she give
instructions that the newspapers were to mention Abdul
Karim more rather than less?

5

The Fatal Christmas Card

In December 1894 Sir Henry Ponsonby's second son Frederick – known as 'Fritz' – joined the Royal Household. Before leaving India, Fritz had been asked to visit the Munshi's father, so that he would be able to report to the Queen on arrival. He had found Waziruddin to be a person of no account, untrained in orthodox medicine. In due course the Queen asked young Ponsonby for his impression of the old gentleman, but when her new Equerry ventured to give it the Queen declared that he must have seen the wrong man!

As A.D.C. to the Viceroy, Lord Elgin, Fritz had known about the Munshi, but only at a distance of several thousand miles. It is clear from a letter penned to his old boss early in 1895 that the topic was not new:

Osborne, Jan 16 1895

Dear Lord Elgin

I find the Munshi is a more difficult question to grapple with than I had thought. I thought that no one here had any idea of what the Munshi really was, but I find that not only all the Household but also Princess Louise P. Beatrice and Prince Henry have been told very clearly about him and what the feeling in India is towards him. Also that they have spoken to the Queen about it and that Lord Rosebery and Fowler have done their best to explain to her the state of affairs. But she won't listen to any of them and thinks they know nothing about it.

Of course I don't know how much they have told her or what they have said but anyhow it has been perfectly useless and the Munshi occupies very much the same

position as John Brown used to. I have been told that both
your and Lady Elgin's letters are given him to read and
that he retails all the news back to India. My father is, as
you know, very ill, so I consulted Sir Fleetwood Edwards
as to whether it would be any good my talking to the
Queen about it, taking the Christmas card sent to you as
an excuse for doing so.

He thought I had better not say anything about it
unless the Queen asked and then only with caution as she
would not listen to me.

There have been two rows lately, one when Edwards
refused to go to tea with the Munshi and the other when
Doctor Reid refused to take the Munshi's father round the
hospitals in London, and in both cases the Queen refused
to listen to what they had to say but was very angry, so as
you see the Munshi is a sort of pet, like a dog or cat which
the Queen will not willingly give up.

Both Edwards and Bigge think that the Queen would
listen to you if you could write and point out to her the
importance of not elevating the Munshi to the position of
a confidential adviser and explain to her what the feeling
in India is with regard to the Munshi. I am certain that
that would be the only chance of getting her to listen.

At the tableaux the Munshi took a very prominent part,
and a seat in the audience next to the Lady in Waiting
(much to her disgust) was reserved for him by order from
the Queen. The Khitmagar on duty helps the Queen to
walk into dinner and even into the chapel here, so you will
see how great is her opinion of all the natives here. I have
now got to think it lucky that the Munshi's sweeper does
not dine with us.[1]

A week later Fritz Ponsonby felt compelled to address Lord
Elgin again:

Osborne, Jan 25th 1895

Dear Lord Elgin
Since I wrote last week the Queen has sent to me and
asked me to find out whether you had received the Xmas
card from the Munshi. I thought this was an excellent

'Fritz' Ponsonby sits cross-legged surrounded by other members of the Royal Household in 1897. Seated at the table is Sir Fleetwood Edwards, and behind him Lord Cross, Secretary of State for India in the 1880s. Sir James Reid is on the far right. Also seated is the Hon. Alexander Yorke, sometimes known as the 'Court Jester', and to the right the Hon. Marie Adeane, Maid of Honour.

opportunity of telling her myself all about the Munshi, but Bigge, Edwards and others strongly opposed my doing so as they thought the Queen would be angry at messages being sent through me, that she would not listen to what I had to say and that it would take away from the effect of your letter.

The Queen's message to me was that I might find out through anyone on the staff or write straight to you so that if you think it best Babbington-Smith or Durand could write to me a letter that I might show. Miss Phipps who is a sort of confidential secretary to the Queen tells me that Lord Harris and Lord Wenlock returned their Xmas cards, at least the Queen told her so. This makes it rather more difficult.

I only see the Queen after dinner when she chooses to

send up for me, so that really I have no opportunity for talking to her. I am certain that if the facts of the case were explained to her by you she would understand.
Yours sincerely
Fritz Ponsonby[2]

Private Secretary's Office Govt. House, Calcutta
13th Feb '95

My dear Fritz
In reply to your letter to the Viceroy I have H.E.'s permission to say that he did receive a Xmas card from Munshi Abdul Karim. He did not imagine that any acknowledgement was necessary, or that the Queen would expect him to send one, and I need scarcely point out to you how impossible it would be for an Indian Viceroy to enter into correspondence of this kind.
Yours sincerely
A. Durand.[3]

The Viceroy did however correspond with an official at the India Office, Whitehall.

February 15 '95 Confidential.

Dear Mr Fowler
I asked Godley to mention to you some time ago that I had received a Xmas card from the Queen's Munshi with a covering letter, and that I did not intend to answer, but had asked young Ponsonby, who has been my A.D.C., to say if asked, that I had received it.
I now enclose some correspondence from which you will see that H.M. is somewhat persistent and I ought to add that in a letter to Lady Elgin she enquired if I had received the card. I am quite ready to write myself if it will do any good. I am, however inclined to doubt it. H.M. would scarcely give up one of her favourite attendants because of anything I could say – and unless she did so little good would result.
If she writes to me direct, not being satisfied with the reply sent through Ponsonby I suppose I should have to speak out plainly, and it is in case this happens that I

The 9th Earl of Elgin, G.C.S.I., K.G., Viceroy of India 1894-99, who did not appreciate receiving the Munshi's Christmas card.

mention these circumstances – because I should be glad to know the position you and Rosebery have taken up and be then guided in my own.

Sincerely

Elgin.[4]

Early the following month, the Viceroy received a letter from London advising him to remember 'that the Queen does show your letters to this gentleman', and to govern himself accordingly. This presented a tricky problem for His Excellency, as he had been wont to write detailed reports to the Queen, knowing she enjoyed them, and if these suddenly became thinner, she would become suspicious.

Little did Abdul Karim know that his Christmas cards to 'the heaven born' had not only been treated with contempt but caused waves of indignation.

Spring that year found the Court at Windsor, after a refreshing holiday spent on the Côte d'Azur where another visitor, Lord Salisbury, received the Queen for tea at his villa 'La Bastide'. Lady Edward Cecil remembered how animated the Queen was, eagerly enjoying the gossip about members of that charmed circle.

> Windsor Castle.
> 15th May 1895
>
> My dear Abdul
> Lady Churchill and Miss Phipps would like to call on 'Mr Munshi' between 12 and *one* and the former choose a kitten. This could then be sent over to Lady Churchill's place near here as soon as it can leave its mother.
> If the weather is like today please come up here at 1/2 past ten. If it should be *Hot* I would telephone down to you not to come up, but to join me at the Tea Cottage.
> Your affectionate Mother VRI[5]

In June 1895 Dr Reid had a conversation with Sir John Tyler, in which Sir John expressed himself with what seems to have been customary frankness. The Queen had created her Munshi Companion of the Order of the Indian Empire – despite stiff opposition from her advisers. The C.I.E. carried no little importance in the Honours system, and was often awarded to higher Civil Servants.

Sir John, in his conversation with Reid, was clearly furious about this break with the usual form, as Reid's diary entry shows, when he reported the gist of what Sir John had said:

A simple meal at Windsor in 1895. With the Queen are Prince and Princess Henry of Battenberg and their three children, attended by *khitmagars* as a footman looks on.

The Munshi Hafiz Abdul
Karim, C.I.E., showing off
his medals in 1895.

The Queen had made a vital mistake in giving the Munshi
the C.I.E., that he is a man of very low origin and of no
education, that he was never anything but a 'Khitmagar'
in which capacity he was sent here; and that the idea of
being considered a gentleman is most ludicrous to those
who know him, that the accounts of him published by
Rafiuddin Ahmed in 'Black and White' and other

magazines were false in almost every particular, and that Rafiuddin Ahmed is a clever but unscrupulous and dangerous man who ought never under any pretext to be admitted to any of the Queen's houses; that he uses the Munshi as a tool for his own purposes; and that when it will serve his purpose, he will be the first man to expose him and turn him into ridicule with the public, wh. he will have no difficulty in doing.[6]

Any supposed danger posed by Rafiuddin seems to have passed by the Queen. Quite probably the Munshi enjoyed using his considerable influence with her to push his friend's career along, and the Queen wasn't slow to respond. As always she chivvied officialdom, instructing her acting Secretary, Arthur Bigge:

Please cypher to Lord Salisbury. Hope you received my letter written two days ago. Since writing I hear that Raffendi [*sic*] Ahmed is most anxious to see you. You know how serious for us in India would be injustice or supposed injustice on our part towards the Moslems, for I have more Mohammedan subjects than the Sultan. Pray see him as soon as you can.[7]

The interview took place on 23rd October 1895, and there may have been more than one. Who was a Prime Minister, after all, to refuse such special pleading? Ultimately, Rafiuddin was destined not to appear in the wider world offered by a diplomatic career, nor is there any reason to believe that the Lord Chancellor furthered his prospects in the Law as the Queen had hoped. Salisbury later intimated to the Queen that he had regrettably found evidence of racial prejudice, which prevented his forwarding Ahmed, managing thus to appear sympathetic to the Queen's views while at the same time absolving himself from guilt. For her part, the Queen most likely saw this transparent excuse for what it was. Disappointed no doubt, but nothing daunted, she would continue to offer Rafiuddin the prestige of invitations to Court Balls. She would accept him, let others think what they liked.

6

The Munshi Triumphant

Whether by chance, or because the Queen wished to further her interest in India, she invited Lady Lytton, widow of a former Viceroy, to be a Lady in Waiting, starting her term of appointment in the autumn of 1895. Lady Lytton's reminiscences, revealed in a Court Diary, show her to have been almost as stiff as the corsets she wore, and one wonders how much true companionship she was able to give her Royal employer.

> October 17th 1895
> Balmoral
>
> A white frost, seven degrees, and the loveliest clearest day I ever saw. It reminded me of the hills in India in October …. Drive with the Queen. Her Majesty spoke of the Munshi for the first time, and wished me to see him and his wife, as 'he was presented to Lord Lytton at Grasse'. My one and only wish is to please the Queen. Then she said she wished the Mohammedans could be let alone by missionaries, and many things in which I disagree, but rather implying she discussed them with the Munshi, which is a risk.[1]

One feels there was very little on which the Queen and Lady Lytton would have agreed.

> Saturday October 19th 1895
>
> The most lovely clear day and warmer. The Queen wished me to go and see Mrs Karim and the Munshi at their house, so Miss Phipps came with me. She is a nice

The Queen with Abdul
Karim, her 'Indian Private
Secretary', whom she had
created C.I.E., describing
him as 'such a very excellent person, so modest,
retiring and exemplary in
his conduct'. In the
Garden Cottage, Balmoral,
October 1895.

little woman and had such pretty native dress and jewels.
He came in very jauntily after a bit and put out his hand
à l'Anglaise, so of course we took it, but we did not sit
down and we did not stay long.

I wrote my name in his book where many Royalties
have written. I wonder what he writes home to his country?[2]

One feels that Lady Lytton only deigned to sign the Visitors Book because Royalties had done so before her. Edith Lytton had something of the superior attitude of the Raj, which the Queen deplored, and it was to escape such a narrow point of view that she liked to discuss Indian affairs with Abdul. She was anxious that the right people should be aware of his importance: an undated letter to Lord George Hamilton, Secretary of State for India, must be one of the most heartfelt the Queen ever wrote:

> The Queen Empress wishes to thank Lord George Hamilton most sincerely for his very kind letter which has been a great relief and satisfaction to her. Her Munshi (and Indian Private Secretary) is such a very excellent person, so modest, retiring and so exemplary in his conduct that the Queen was very anxious Lord George Hamilton should understand his confidential tho' unpolitical position so as to be able to put down and contradict any false reports etc. especially in India itself .... The Queen hoped her having an Indian adviser would give satisfaction – misapprehensions might have arisen.

Karim Cottage, the Munshi's 'snug abode' at Balmoral.

Sir Henry Ponsonby,
Queen Victoria's Private
Secretary for thirty years.
At his death in 1895 the
Queen said that he had
been 'above all prejudice
and narrowness' and like a
second father to her 'good
Munshi'.

Munshi Abdul Karim is most useful to her in many
ways for his discretion and intelligence.

It is also useful to hear what Indians themselves feel
which she fears is rarely the case at the India Office and
even at the Viceroy's Court, where the Viceroy hears
nothing but Anglo Indian insults ....[3]

Her Majesty's Yacht "Alberta" entering Cowes Harbour.

Dr Reid inscribed this photograph of the Royal Yacht *Alberta* for his scrapbook, 1884.

After thirty years devoted service to the Crown, Sir Henry Ponsonby died in November 1895. Greatly moved, but relieved 'his spirit freed from the bondage of a poor suffering body' the Queen wrote to her 'beloved and darling child', the Empress Frederick of Germany: Sir Henry's death had been felt by no one more than her 'good Munshi' to whom he had been like a second father. She felt he had been 'above all prejudice and narrowness which, alas, is not the case with everyone'.[4]

The Munshi's power and influence were now at their zenith; his status had become almost mythical, as the following press report shows:

DECEMBER 19 1895

ABDUL KARIM
The Queen's Munshi Follows his Sovereign to Osborne

The Munshi Abdul Karim came to England as the Queen's personal attendant and instructor in Hindustani. Her Majesty having acquired the language, has promoted Abdul Karim to be her private secretary for India, and he now occupies a position as regards India corresponding to

Arthur Cottage, Abdul
Karim's residence at
Osborne.

that held for the United Kingdom by the late Sir Henry
Ponsonby. He has his own apartments, his personal staff,
and is admitted to the drawing room with the gentlemen
of the Court. No longer does the Queen rest upon his arm
when moving from room to room, but she rests upon his
judgement when she is in communication with the subject
princes of the Great Empire beyond the seas, and Abdul
Karim

Knows His Own Importance

Yesterday the Queen travelled from Windsor to Osborne. So did Abdul Karim. For the Sovereign the Alberta
was the detailed yacht, for the dusky secretary the Elfin.
Like his Sovereign he is a stickler for secrecy; and like her,
too, he is very human. He never travels without his Scotch
attendant; he has a horror of salutes; and though he
courts ceremony it must not be ostentatious. The Queen
has her animal attachments, and the donkey is her
favourite; the Munshi takes a lower-ground, but his cat
and his canary go with him wheresoever he travels.

Last night Abdul Karim sat with Oriental patience in a
railway carriage at the Harbour station for full twenty
minutes, chatting with his wife and mother-in-law until

he could walk straight from the train to the Elfin, as the latter

With Royal Dignity

would not go alongside the harbour Pier until the Cowes and Ryde boats had quitted the scene. The tide was as rebellious as the Susan of the play, and the Elfin had to back and fill for a long time before she could be berthed without damaging her figurehead.

Ultimately steam had conquered the tide, and as soon as the Elfin was berthed Staff-Commander G.A. Broad approached the railway carriage to inform Abdul Karim that the coast was clear. The Scotchman, with tall hat, and without the slightest vestige of Celtic insignia beyond what was revealed in his accents, piloted the cat and canary through the damp and fog of the night to the yacht, and the Munshi, with his female relatives, followed, with Captain Broad in attendance. The Munshi stands some six feet in height, speaks broken English in a melodious voice, and interprets to his

Wife and Mother-in-Law

who are so veiled and draped as to resemble moving automata, and as they pass down to the Elfin they vanish out of the sight of the porters, who are the only spectators of the passage of the singular Oriental who has a rooted antipathy to the gaze of the vulgar. Yet to look upon his face and to hear his voice one would think the Munshi could tame lions and silence tigers. But he has an exalted position and fully recognises his own importance. For the Munshi is the only member of the Queen's personal staff who is allowed to travel in semi-regal state.[5]

Suspicion of Abdul Karim had not been entirely allayed. Early in 1896 the Munshi sailed for India. Government circles were somewhat apprehensive that he might use his time there in support of dissidents who were many and various, united only by their hatred of British Rule. Lord George Hamilton saw fit to establish with the Viceroy the attitude that should be adopted in surveillance.

A Victorian view of India. This tableau vivant, performed on 5th and 6th October 1888, features Princess Beatrice as 'India' attended by her nieces Princess Louise of Wales (holding box) and Princess Alix of Hesse. Around them, from left to right: Khairat Ali, Abdul Karim, Mohammed Bukhsh and Abdul Hussain.

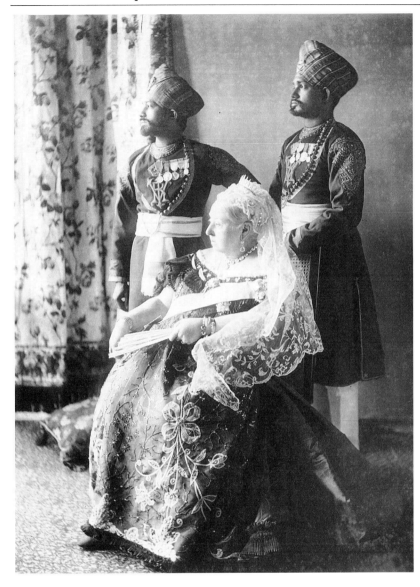

Victoria Regina et Imperatrix, with Mustafa and Chidda, 1896.

February 21 1896
To Lord Elgin

I think that you would be justified in keeping such general notice of his proceedings as to enable you to determine whether or not anything unusual is going on and if there are signs of a propaganda of intrigue to have recourse to closer supervision, considering the resentment a knowledge of such supervision would cause. It would be better to err on the side of laxity than of vigour of watch at first. If there is nothing unusual or objectionable in his proceedings I should be disposed to make the watch unconstant.

By treating him in the first instance only with the care any visitor of importance would obtain, you supply yourself with a satisfactory answer if questioned by a high authority, and there might be a risk of a summary order to exempt from supervision if your cautious action was too noticeable. Any order of that kind would become known, and do more harm to the authority of the Indian Government than any amount of underhand intrigue. The older anyone becomes the less reasonable they are to argument in anything affecting the personality of a favourite.

Believe me yours very truly.[6]   Hamilton

Off duty: Lord Elgin with 'Flink' and 'Tim', photographed by his daughter, Lady Christian Bruce, 16th May 1896.

The fear of a summary order to exempt him from supervision shows how aware Ministers of the Crown were of the Queen's iron will and her power to influence events.

> Government House, Calcutta – From the Viceroy to
> Lord Sandhurst
> March 14th 1896
>
> The Munshi is coming out. I am not sure about the exact date, but about this time. I have consulted Hamilton whether it was necessary to do anything in the way of watching his movements. The result is that we do not wish to watch him, only we should like to know if any of the intriguers whose operations in Native States and elsewhere we are obliged to watch, make any attempt to approach him. It would be inexpedient to 'shadow' him, or indeed to take any step that could be built up as a source of distrust of himself personally, but D. Ethbridge whom I saw this morning ... saw no difficulty about obtaining general information about visitors and the like.
>
> In speaking of what was necessary in Bombay where it would be highly probable that he would be met by some of the gentlemen to whom I have referred – it occurred to me that it would be better for me to write to you personally – so that no written instructions need issue to any police officer. My object therefore is to ask you to do what you can with as little stir as possible.
>
> I do not think we desire more than what is sent up to us as a matter of course if a man happens to have a Russian or other suspicious name.
>
> I was amused the other day to find in one of these Reports an account of some length of the personal appearance and movements of a gentleman who came here with a letter of introduction from my brother-in-law who is one of the Secretaries of the Embassy at S. Petersburg! All that is wanted is similar vigilance in this case, and the more it is made to seem a matter of ordinary routine the better.
>
> You will easily understand that mistaken zeal in this case might easily do far more harm than good, and wd. be capable of any amount of misrepresentation.[7]

Thus far had the Munshi risen, from Clerk in Agra jail at 10 Rupees a month. It appears that his visit to India was uneventful.

'Dear Osborne', Queen Victoria's favourite home, its design influenced by Prince Albert.

The Queen's cosy sitting-room-cum-study at Osborne.

7

A Year of Battles

In 1897, a year after the Munshi's quiet visit to India, the Court was seething with animosity towards him. Positions had become more deeply entrenched; open quarrels flared up between the Queen and her Household. This turbulent period soon became more intense than ever.

Accustomed to spending early spring in the South of France – as did many other crowned heads at that time, the Queen and her entourage were to occupy an entire wing of the Hotel Excelsior Regina, Cimiez (named after its illustrious guest), which was rented for 50,000 Francs. Thither the Household decamped; and as much of the Royal furniture was transported

The Grand Hotel, Grasse, 1891, one of Queen Victoria's springtime retreats.

there too it was very much a home from home. There was plenty to interest visitors each year with local festivals. The Battle of Flowers was held at the end of March, in the square in front of the convent church in Cimiez. In nearby Menton there would be the Fête des Citrons, filling the streets with scents of lemon and orange, with the town band, all swagger and showmanship, thumping out lively tunes.

The Queen took daily rides along the promenade, and excursions in her donkey cart to the picturesque villages amongst the hills; to Grasse, for instance, where she enjoyed Alice de Rothschild's delightful garden. The Queen, when staying in Grasse, was a frequent visitor at Miss Alice's 'Villa Victoria', so named by permission. In the evening the Royal guest would ask Alice to go and sit with her. On one occasion, Lady Battersea, a Rothschild cousin and a guest at the villa, was also invited to the Grand Hotel. They found the Queen sitting in a small room, listening while at work to Princess Beatrice, who was playing duets on the piano with the Queen's maid-of-honour, Marie Adeane, Her Majesty beating time with her crochet hook.

Apparently, when speaking privately, the Queen invariably referred to Alice de Rothschild as 'The All-Powerful One' on account of her energy. This found expression in the continual enlargement of the 'mountain garden', a wonder to the Queen, who often traversed it in her donkey-chair.

If the surroundings were all sunlight and tranquillity, the emotional temperature within the Queen's Household was thundery. It was from Fritz Ponsonby that the news broke, in a letter to Sir Henry Babbington-Smith, Private Secretary to the Viceroy.

> Hotel Excelsior Regina, Cimiez
> April 27th 1897
>
> My dear Babs
> Thank you so much for your 2 letters, and the following is strictly confidential, so please treat it like the confessional. We have been having a good deal of trouble lately about the Munshi here, and although we have tried our best we cannot get the Queen to realise how very dangerous it is for her to allow this man to see every confidential

paper relating to India, in fact to all State affairs. The Queen insists on bringing the Munshi forward, and if it were not for our protest, I don't know where she would stop. Fortunately he seems to be a thoroughly stupid and uneducated man, and his one idea in life seems to be to do nothing and to eat as much as he can.

I don't know whether you remember a man of the name Rafiuddin Ahmed, who tried to stand for Parliament. Well he supplies the brains which are deficient in the Munshi, and being a very clever man, he tries to extract all he can out of the Munshi, and that I think is where the real danger comes in. The Munshi is even allowed to read the Viceroy's letters, and any letters of importance that come from India. Things have now come to such a pass that the police have been consulted and have furnished some rather interesting details about the Munshi and Rafiuddin.

But it is of no use, for the Queen says that it is 'race prejudice' and that we are all jealous of the poor Munshi (!)

Now what I should be very grateful if you could do is to send me any cuttings from the native or European papers bearing on this vexed question. I got hold of some from the Hindoo papers before I left India, and had them read to the Queen, but their contents did very little good. Now however as the question has arisen with such force, it would be of the greatest use to be able to quote Indian papers.

She has found one or two people who would say anything to please her to back her up. Chiefly Lord Breadalbane, who as I learnt a short time ago wants to be Viceroy.[1]

To understand what had led up to Fritz Ponsonby's conspiratorial letter, we have to go back about a month. At the end of March 1897, Prince Louis of Battenberg, who acted as liaison between the Queen and Household, had been sent to Arthur Davidson, Groom-in-Waiting, to convey Her Majesty's wish that the Gentlemen should associate more with Abdul Karim. The Household took such exception to this Royal command that they threatened to resign if the Queen pressed the matter.

On 30th March, Dr Reid was called in to see the Queen many times on account of the crisis. There were comings and goings, Prince Louis having conversations with the more senior Household members. The Queen was volatile, showing some signs of giving way under pressure, but still taking the Munshi's part and protecting him.

Early in April, Dr Reid, who was shortly to be made a Baronet, began a series of stressful interviews with the Queen, who expressed her emotions in a sequence of long letters following these confrontations with her doctor. Reid, meticulous Scotsman that he was, kept a diary record of the substance of all that passed between himself, others in the Household, and the Queen.

As someone in whom the Queen confided, Reid was deemed the ideal person to convey the profound unease felt about the Queen's preferment of the Munshi. His diary entry for April 4th 1897 records his advice:

> It seems to me that Your Majesty is only thinking of the Munshi's feelings: but that is of infinitesimal importance compared with the gravity of the situation as regards Your Majesty. As I said to your Majesty before, there are people in high places, who know Your Majesty well, who say to me that the only charitable explanation that can be given is that Your Majesty is not sane, and that the time will come when to save Your Majesty's memory and reputation it will be necessary for me to come forward and say so: and that is a nice position for me to be in. I have seen the Prince of Wales yesterday and he again spoke to me very seriously on the subject.
>
>   He says he has quite made up his mind to come forward if necessary, because quite apart from all the consequences to the Queen, it affects himself most vitally …. Because it affects the throne.[2]

Matters had not improved on the following day:

> A very painful interview with the Queen, who got into a most violent passion and said we had all behaved disgracefully.[3]

One of Queen Victoria's
many walking sticks, with
its beautifully shaped gold
handle, and mementos which
came into the possession of
Sir James Reid: a lock of
Queen Victoria's hair, her
watch and her smelling salts.

As if this volatile situation were not enough, trouble had
been exacerbated by the reappearance of Rafiuddin Ahmed,
who no doubt hoped to enjoy some social cachet on the Riviera
and other obvious advantages of the location. His arrival was
ill-judged, and the Household combined to send Raffuddin out
of the Munshi's orbit. However, the days following his departure were extremely stormy.

The press, as ever, cast a sardonic eye over the scene, still
with some ambiguity about Abdul, as this quixotic piece from
the *Galignani Messenger*, Nice, shows:

Both in Italy and on the Riviera the Queen of England's
Indian attendants excite the greatest interest and curios-
ity. They are supposed to be a living proof of the might of
Britain's empire beyond the seas.

As for the Munshi Abdul Kareem, although every def-
erence is paid to him, and he is generally seen following
the Royal carriage in a separate carriage drawn by splendid horses, each Niçois is firmly convinced that he sees in

him a captive Native prince, attached, as it were, to the chariot-wheels of the Empress of India.[4]

Had the Munshi become this mythic figure in little more than ten years? If the Queen's continued favour by turns surprised, exasperated and intrigued the world at large, the Munshi himself must have been well aware of his extraordinary power. Maybe, like his friend Raffiudin, he too was something of a chameleon, accepting the position of which the notable carriage with equipage was a symbol.

News of the debacle in Cimiez spread to Whitehall.

India Office, Whitehall. From Lord George Hamilton,
Secretary of State for India

Confidential   April 30th 1897

Dear Lord Elgin

Since I got your last letter there is little of confidential character to write about; but there is some Court commotion going on as to the position and conduct of the Munshi, of which I better give you an account. The Household generally, especially the private secretaries, much resent the social and official position accorded to him in the Court Circular and on all occasions by the Queen.

So far as I know the Munshi has done nothing to my knowledge which is reprehensible or deserving of official stricture, but he does consort very much with a Mohammedan intriguer named Rafiuddin who is known to the secret police in India as an untrustworthy adventurer and is, I believe, the agent of the Amir here.

At Cimiez he and the Munshi have, I understand, been living in the same house, and whether it is in consequence of this or not I do not know, but anyhow a row occurred – Sir A. Bigge representing to the Queen that the Munshi's position etc were far in excess of what they ought to be.

In consequence I telegraphed for some facts as to the status of his family – since then Fleetwood Edwards came to see me and told me that a row was impending and that the Munshi's intercourse with Rafiuddin was becoming closer and closer, and that he was not in his opinion a fit

person to be hand in glove with the Queen's Munshi, and
he asked me if I had any information as to Rafiuddin's
character and antecedents. I told him that I had, and
referred him to Lee-Warner whom I told to give all the
information he had and to obtain if he could more. This he
has done by writing two letters of 9th and 18th April to
Mr Bayley .... They are just capable of the interpretation
that inquiries should be set on foot about the Munshi's
character and past proceedings. This I do not want done.
I don't want to get mixed up in any Court mudpies unless
the Queen directly appeals to me; inquiries should be
made as regards Rafiuddin, and if it is clearly shown, as
I think it can be, that he is a disreputable fellow, making
money out of his association with the Munshi, then it
might be my duty to make such a statement to the Queen.

I do not however want any fishing enquiry to be made
in connection with the Munshi, as such enquiries would
not be right, unless they were in association with some
definite statement or accusation. I shall hear more in a
day or two as the Court have come back from the South of
France, but whatever may be the outcome of this little
storm, I am sure that the influence of the Munshi will
hereafter be in decline.[5]

One feels that Hamilton's wish was father to the thought.
Events were to prove him wrong.

Lord Elgin replied from Simla on 18th May 1897, saying
that he had seen two letters sent by Sir William Lee-Warner
for the attention of A. Bayley (Thuggee and Dacoity department), furnishing all information currently available on Rafiuddin. Acccording to the Viceroy, nothing of note had emerged
from these. His letter continues:

As to the other gentleman, I asked if it could be shown in
your words, 'that he is a disreputable fellow making
money out of his connection with the Munshi'. He said no,
there was absolutely no proof – there was not even a pool
to fish in. We certainly believe that you rightly describe
him, but we have no facts. I remember MacDonnell when,
as Home Member I consulted him in 1894, pointing out to
me that if it was desired to watch correspondence, that

must be done at the point of origin. Once it gets into the post office it is impossible to say what channel it may be flowing in – and I fancy no-one would suggest that we should establish a sort of censorship of all letters passing by the ordinary post from India. I need not say that I entirely agree that the evil, if possible, should be removed. At the same time I much doubt the existence of great political danger. There may be a certain amount of intrigue and corruption, but I do not believe this sort of agent has enough influence to make himself dangerous.[6]

In early summer of that year, there was evidently a move afoot, instigated by the Queen, to promote the Munshi's standing. Two years earlier she had made him a Commander of the Indian Empire. Now it seems she was contemplating a higher honour – that of Knight Commander of the Indian Empire, K.C.I.E. Not surprisingly this caused some raised eyebrows in Whitehall.

From Lord George Hamilton to the Viceroy, 14th May 1897

Dear Lord Elgin
I have to thank you for your letter of 21st ultimo.
Honours, especially in the higher grades, seem to be in a somewhat different category in India to what they are in this country. Here it is a recognition of the individual for work done for the State or Sovereign. In India it is a class distinction and in a country where caste and status are socially all powerful. If the Queen had pressed on me a further recognition of the Munshi's services to her I should have felt some difficulty in opposing her views from the British standpoint, as yearly we elevate and individually elevate for political and other works persons of humble origin. But the objection you urge, that to include him in the higher grade of the I.E. would be to greatly depreciate that grade in the eyes of past graduates, and to subject the reigning princes to an indignity by being made junior to him, as he became of the senior Knights, are conclusive, and though I do not think the request will be made I will certainly decline it if made.[7]

There is no record that the Queen took the matter any further.

Not so, however, in respect of the Royal Victorian Order, the coveted honour awarded for personal services to the Sovereign. Abdul Karim had so worked his way into the Queen's affections that he felt able to ask her favour without embarrassment. Thus he proposed himself for this exclusive distinction. The Queen's Household blocked it quite openly; Sir Fleetwood Edwards, Keeper of the Privy Purse, wrote in terms which left her in no doubt as to their feelings.

The Queen responded, sending one of her customary letters to Dr Reid:

I must own that I am very indignant at this unnecessary letter from Sir F. Edwards. He threatens me in such a way that he almost makes it impossible for me to do what I feel in not doing I should break my written word. This set at me makes my position a very painful and cruel one, and I never shall get over it with the Gentlemen or the pain wh. it caused the poor Munshi. I am crushed and annoyed at Sir Fleetwood's letter ....[8]

Reid was asked to sound out Prime Minister, Lord Salisbury, on the subject. Salisbury was negative. The Queen dashed off another note:

Pray tell Sir Fleetwood Edwards that it was not because of his rather impertinent letter that the Queen does not at present give the Munshi the CVO, but on the advice of Lord Salisbury.[9]

As Reid recorded in May 1897:

Queen much 'mortified' about Munshi but more reasonable.[10]

Pressure had forced her to hesitate, but not, as we shall see, finally to give up.

Relationships were strained, not only in the ranks of the Royal Household, but also apparently among the other Indian servants. One Ahmed Hussain was very free with his feelings about the Munshi when prompted by Reid:

> Munshi always wants more, and every day ask Queen plenty thing. Queen give him too much and plenty present and too much money. India Rajah very angry Munshi get C.I.E., when Rajah and big Indian man not get, and Munshi very little man like Queen footman and some Queen footman better man. He tell me all Englishmen cross, but he say I fight all and Queen always help me. I tell Munshi much better you quiet. You only 10 year servant, very little man in India, and your Father very little doctor, your brother and sister husband very little servant man and policemans. Queen give you plenty money and everything plenty give. Queen never give so much English servant or English Gentleman. Plenty English servant and English Gentleman with Queen 15, 20 years and get nothing, not English custom. But Queen give you very much money, and recommendation for brother and sister husband, and big house, and the land. You better quiet and not always ask Queen and want be big officer.[11]

The Queen's Diamond Jubilee celebrations came and went in June, with a great surge of popular affection which touched her profoundly. Yet despite the public esteem she enjoyed at this time, her private thoughts about the Munshi appear to have been in tumult.

Four months had passed since the events at Cimiez which had been so painful to her, and there was more to come. In July further accusations were brought against the Munshi. The Queen responded with great agitation in a long letter to Reid:

> You say it is of no importance, but the feeling that the poor M. is distracted and anything can be invented against him and that he is suspected by jealous people of being dishonest is extremely trying and painful to me. She [the Queen] has known him for 10 years intimately and certainly has never had any reason to suspect or doubt him.
>
>   The fact of its being believed that he was the cause of the footman Bagley not being promoted shows how ready

The Royal Household with members of the Imperial Suite during the
Tsar's visit to Balmoral in September 1896. Back row: Mlle Wassiltchik-
off, Col. William Carington, Count Worontzoff Daschkoff, Sir Arthur
Bigge, Dr James Reid, Gen. Stanley Clarke, Sir Arthur Davidson. Middle:
Lady Churchill, Lady Lytton, M. de Staal, the Hon. Harriet Phipps, Count
Benckendorff. Front: Lord Pembroke, Prince Galitzyn, Victor Churchill,
Lord Edward Clinton, and possibly M. Dubreuil Eschapper.

everyone is to injure him. The M. never mentioned
Bagley's name or ever mentioned any one of the footmen
or of my other servants. But he is kind in trying to help

others in trouble. The Queen has constantly, long before the M. came, chosen people herself on enquiry, but these Gentlemen wish to have it all in their own hands, and in their hatred of the unfortunate Munshi, put all down to him. It is very offensive that I should always be supposed to be *made* to do things.

I began this letter some days ago but go on today after the very painful conversation I had with you this afternoon. I must go on. If people believe the story about Bagley which is *completely false* may they not believe any painful story brought against this poor defenceless man.

Orientals invent and are of the most ubounded jealousy. The hatred of Hindu against Muhammedan only adds to this. They talk to the Officers, A.D.C.s and Anglo-Indians who readily believe and retail everything. I do think it very shameful of people connected with the Govt. or the Court to give ready credence to these stories of a person in my service. The position of *doubt* is becoming quite intolerable to me.

I *must* have it out with my poor friend. If there have been imprudences and faults it may, I should hope, be possible to put a stop to this, and so let the poor M. redeem his character. It is impossible for me not to feel the position as most offensive towards me. I can't bear it.[12]

Feeling thus undermined, the Queen's reaction was to turn her attention again to the possibility of advancement for Rafiuddin, with several heartfelt letters to Lord Salisbury. In July she was worrying that Ahmed might have been hurt by his expulsion from Cimiez, saying that she feared 'we did act wrongly in treating him as a suspected person of which we had no proofs ….'[13]

Might not Ahmed be employed in getting information from Mohammedans which would be useful to the Government, the Queen wondered? In August she asked Lord Salisbury to apologise to Rafiuddin for his dismissal from the South of France, expressing her own conviction that '... he had done nothing to displease or offend the Queen'. A few weeks later, the Queen heard from Salisbury that suspicions against Rafiuddin had been 'unjust' – even the Editor of the *Nineteenth Century*, to which Ahmed contributed, had testified that he was 'much too honourable' to give information.[14] In the end it seemed the case against him had collapsed.

The Queen also wrote unequivocally about the Munshi's supposed closeness to confidential State papers:

> With reference to the subject on which Lord Salisbury has been so kind & just – the Queen would just wish to assert that *no* political papers of any kind are ever in the Munshi's hands *even* in her presence. He only helps her to read words which she cannot read or merely ordinary submissions on warrants for signature. He does not read English fluently enough to be able to read anything of importance.[15]

Unless doubt is to be cast on the Queen's word, it seems that this issue too had been exaggerated by the Munshi's enemies.

8

The Chill Winds of Autumn

The issue of the Queen's relationship with the Munshi and her Household was still painfully alive in the autumn at Balmoral. It appears that Abdul Karim had been upset enough to threaten the Queen with resignation. Fearing the severance of a relationship on which she had come to depend, the Queen gave vent to her feelings obsessively. There's every reason to see why she felt undermined.

> Balmoral
> 8th September '97
>
> I am much troubled at the M's expressed determination or rather decided wish not to remain beyond this year. He says everything can be enquired and looked to, and that all receipts will be forthcoming but that he is not of the nature to endure such treatment which he has experienced.
>
> Of course I feel and understand what his feelings must be, for I feel deeply hurt at what has occurred since March and it has always been present in my mind. I told him I cd. not let him go, and that it besides would do him and me much harm.
>
> He would appear to admit the accusation and I to have yielded to very shameful pressure.[1]

More than six months after the first storm over the Munshi in Cimiez came the climax at chilly Balmoral. The catalyst was a piece of self-promotion by the Munshi, in which he was as adept as ever. This coup was in the form of a photograph in the Diamond Jubilee edition of the *Graphic*. Showing the Queen seated at her table, dog at her feet, attended by her Indian Secretary as she signed documents, the caption read: 'The Queen's Life in the Highlands. Her Majesty receiving a lesson in Hindustani from the Munshi Hafiz Abdul Karim C.I.E.'

Unperturbed though the Queen might be (and she appears to have been quite content initially), the Household was deeply displeased. The newly honoured doctor, Sir James Reid, had an interview with the Queen about 'the offending photograph', and in his own words made her feel 'rather uncomfortable'.[2]

The story now assumes the desperation reminiscent of a silent movie. Reid cycled off to Ballater and saw the photographer, Milne, who confirmed that the Munshi had ordered publication of the said photograph. Speeding back to Balmoral on the velocipede, Sir James then told the Queen all, which lead to three 'painful' interviews with her. The distraught Queen afterwards penned a note:

> Pray do not see Milne if he comes. The Munshi tells me he has written to Milne and wants to see him. There is a great deal of indignation about your going to see and question him, which is most unfortunate and you should not have done it without telling me, as it may now produce very painful consequences for me as the Munshi looks on you as his bitter enemy.[3]

Subequently the Queen declared herself to be 'terribly annoyed and upset by all this stupid business'. Her loyalty was such that she couldn't bring herself to doubt the Indian, but the issue went wider. A great deal of pressure had been brought to bear. As the Queen wrote:

> I feel continually aggrieved at my Gentlemen wishing to spy upon and interfere with one of my people whom I have no personal reason or proof of doubting, and I am greatly distressed at what has happened ....[4]

So far from doubting Abdul, the Queen was beginning to doubt the good faith of her doctor and hitherto confidential adviser. No wonder she felt insecure, admitting to 'feeling dreadfully nervous'.[5]

Meanwhile, what impact was the Munshi now making out-

Abdul Karim with his
nephew, Abdul Raschid, in
1897.

side Court circles? The following report appeared in the *World*
on 15th September 1897:

> The Munshi Abdul Karim who now occupies his own snug
> abode in the grounds of Balmoral, has received extraordi-

nary rapid promotion since he came to Windsor in the capacity of 'personal attendant' to her Majesty in 1887.

He was then only four-and-twenty, and as a clerk at Agra only earned a pound a month. He soon commenced giving lessons in Hindustani to the Queen, who now not only speaks that language fluently, but can write it with more than average correctness in the Persian character.

So devoted is Her Majesty to her oriental studies that when the Munshi went to India on leave, they were continued by almost daily correspondence. About seven years ago the Munshi was joined by his wife, and his father Waziruddin is certainly the only man living who has been permitted to smoke a hookah in the room usually tenanted by Lord Salisbury when he visits Windsor Castle.

Frogmore Cottage has been assigned to Abdul Karim as a residence, and it is now full of souvenirs and presents of all sorts, including a gold and enamel tea service, the gift of the Emperor of Russia. His place as 'personal attendant' is now filled by his compatriots Mustapha Khan and Chota Khan of Agra, and Aziz Khan of Maradebad [sic]; and when Her Majesty dines, lunches or breakfasts en famille, no other servant is present but her faithful Indians, with whom she can speak in their own language.[6]

The old year finished as it had started, chronicled in Reid's diary:

Christmas Day 1897

Before dinner had a most stormy talk for three quarters of an hour with Queen about Munshi. H.M. quite mad with rage, but I stood my ground firmly. Dined with the Queen ....[7]

9

A Prince Manqué

The Munshi did not resign. Intrigue amongst courtiers, though not at an end, appears to have become more subdued, and the Queen's overwrought nerves to have been soothed. Perhaps the intense feelings which had come out in her confrontations with Reid and subsequent letters had been defused. Much passion had been spent, and for a time it seems that the atmosphere was calmer.

In January 1898, the figure of Rafiuddin Ahmed was still shadowing Abdul Karim, though in more substantial form he was attending rallies of the Muslim League.

Dadabhai Nairoji had become the first Indian to be elected to the House of Commons in 1892, when he took his seat as Liberal member for Finsbury Central, an East London constituency. He had won by only five votes over his Conservative opponent. He now featured in a statement to the press claiming that Rafiuddin had taken part in 'disloyal demonstrations', which the latter of course denied. It was enough, however, to stir renewed suspicion about Ahmed, and Sir Ernest Bradford, Chief of the Metropolitan Police, was detailed to keep him under surveillance.

There is a certain amount of confusion as to what was actually going on; the facts are few, but it is certain that there was a meeting of the Muslim Patriotic League on 10th January 1898, at which Raffiudin took the chair, when 'loyal resolutions' were passed. This seems to have been the cue for Nairoji to communicate with *The Times*, asserting that on 29th December 1897, at a prior meeting of the Muslim League, Rafiuddin had taken part in disloyal manifestations 'which he now pretended to deplore'. To this accusation, Rafiuddin replied that he 'had only been present as a spectator'.[1]

There really does not apppear to be much evidence, if any, that Rafiuddin Ahmed was a danger to the State. Lord Elgin had confidently given that opinion. Yet Sir James Reid and others seem to have been obsessed with the possible threat he posed to security. The assumption seems to have had more to do with Rafiuddin's appearance – he was a swarthy bearded figure – than with any objective reality. Reid, however, felt it incumbent on himself to write to Lord Salisbury:

> PRIVATE AND CONFIDENTIAL
> Osborne
> 29th January 1898
>
> Pray pardon my intruding on you about a matter which I think you had better know. It seems to me to be very probable that the Munshi may wish to take his friend Rafiuddin about with him, to be his companion at Cimiez and, should he urge this on the Queen, I believe Her Majesty might consent, as she has of late been getting you to think well of Rafiuddin, and as believing that all suspicions about him are groundless.
>
> Now what I think you know, is that Sir Ernest Bradford, the Head of the Police, who has held high appointments in India, knows something of Rafiuddin, and entertains an unfavourable opinion of him and of his capacity for mischief. Should you think this a matter of importance, it has occurred to me that you might think it well sometime to see Sir Ernest and hear what he says. At all events you would be getting an unbiased and unprejudiced opinion from an authority of conspicuous probity on a question which seems not unlikely to lead to further trouble than we have had already.[2]

Meanwhile the Queen was trying to ensure that Rafiuddin would not suffer from the opprobium of the previous year – the 'disgraceful affair' as she termed it – and was keen to reinstate him on the guest list for a Ball.[3] What had Rafiuddin done to win the favour of his Sovereign lady? It seems likely that he helped her with Hindustani, augmenting the Munshi's daily lessons. As a highly educated person, Rafiuddin would have

The 3rd Marquess of Salisbury, whom the Queen thought 'so kind and just' about Abdul Karim. Lord Salisbury formed the last of his three governments in 1895. Drawing by Violet Granby, later Duchess of Rutland.

been well able to hold his own in distinguished company, which may have been a source of annoyance to his enemies.

Queen Victoria's Court had been quite unable to diminish the Munshi or his publicist, a fact which rankled profoundly.

Now, late in her life, the Queen was trying to ensure that Abdul Karim would benefit when she was no longer there to protect him.

Osborne   12th February 1898

I have in my Testamentary arrangements secured your comfort and have constantly thought of you well. The long letter I enclose which was written nearly a month ago is *entirely* and solely *my own idea, not a human being will ever* know of it or what you answer me. If you can't read it I will help you and then burn it at *once*.

Your faithful true friend,   VRI[4]

This letter, along with virtually all the Queen's correspondence with Abdul Karim, was burned on the orders of her successor. The fragments which escaped show a tantalising glimpse of what must surely have been a remarkable testament to their friendship.

In due course, Reid and Salisbury met to discuss the contents of Reid's letter. Apparently the Queen had given in to the pressure exerted by her Household sufficiently to pronounce that there was no question of Rafiuddin Ahmed once again going to Cimiez, a decision which Lord Salisbury had underlined. In Sir James Reid's verbatim account of their conversation, the Prime Minister continues:

I have seen Bradford's papers about him, and the worst thing that is certain is that he associates with people who are certainly disloyal – I told H.M. this, and she said 'but he does not sympathise with them'.[5]

It was Reid's opinion that

though R. might now pose as loyal ... a time might come when he would turn round, and make use of weapons he was now accumulating. S. said yes – he quite agreed with me – and added 'I told the Queen that it would be most unfortunate if the French press got hold of anything and turned her into ridicule, and that this was an additional reason for not having R. there. She quite saw this, and seemed impressed by it, and I am quite sure ... that this is the argument to use with her.'[6]

The most perceptive comment Salisbury made during his talk with Reid was in realising that the Queen subconsciously probably enjoyed the emotional frisson generated by the Mun-shi, including the rows, 'being the only form of excitement she can have'.[7] There is no doubt much truth in this, but there certainly does also appear to be an element of cruelty in the way the Queen's Household made known their feelings about the Munshi and his associate.

Spring 1898, and time for departure to the South of France again. The excursions to Cimiez had become an annual event, which the Queen looked forward to. After a hard English winter, the warmth was kind to old rheumaticky bones. The Indian servants would ease her gently into chairs and settle her in a donkey-cart for the daily drives along those quiet country roads just inland from the coast, through lanes of mimosa, abundant citrus groves and almond trees in blossom. Talented and dedicated artist that she was, in earlier days the Queen had taken her watercolours, to portray for her own satisfaction the landscape that attracted Monet and Cézanne. Now in the evening of her life, nearly blind, she could only carry pictures in her head, although she wore strong spectacles in an attempt to improve her vision.

In old age the Queen enjoyed music as much as she had ever done. In June she heard Jean de Reszke in Gounod's *Roméo et Juliette*, given for her at Windsor. She often asked for concerts, with 'Signor Tosti' at the piano to accompany leading artists: Calvé appeared that summer, Gounod and Massenet the favoured composers. In September the Big Top came to Balmoral, when 'Lord' George Sanger brought his celebrated Circus, including 'Koh-i-Nor' the Wonder Horse!

Lady Curzon was summoned to Windsor with her husband in November 1898, before sailing for India, and a letter to her parents recalls how the Queen walked in with her Indian attendant, and the ensuing conversation:

> The Queen received me in a room all hung with mini-atures & made me sit by her, and talked about babies, Indian life & every sort of thing – kissed me again when I left and told me to write her from Marseilles how we all were. Also to write to her from India. Then George had his audience and she gave him my Indian order which I can only wear after he is Viceroy. The order is very pretty indeed of diamonds turquoises & pearls .... Nothing could

Balmoral Castle, 17th June, 1898.

Lord George Sanger's Circus Company.

BY SPECIAL COMMAND
OF
Her Most Gracious Majesty Queen Victoria.
PERFORMANCE COMMENCING AT 3.30.

...PROGRAMME...

1. Overture by the Magnificent Band. Conductor, E. Scholz.
2. Harry Austin will Ride, Drive, and Manage Four Beautiful Coloured Horses.
3. Acrobatic Violinists, by the Bros. Crippin.
4. The Wonderful Clairvoyant and Talking Horse. Introduced by Herr Lancelot. Trained by Lord George Sanger.
5. Mdlle. Ida Evilo in her Daring Trapeze Performance.
6. Performing Horse and Pony, trained and introduced by Herr Nimsi.
7. The Toledas in their Extraordinary Wire Show and Mdlle. Yetta.
8. Beautiful Menage Horse, "Lord Chieftain," introduced by Mons. Arnold.
9. Mdlle. Lilian, the Charming Equestrienne. (Clown, the Great James Holloway).
10. The Eccentric Mule.
11. The Bros. Holloway. Extraordinary Performance on the Double Ladders.
12. Mdlle. Violetta in her Graceful Trotting Act. (Clown, the Original Little Sandy).
13. Six Spotted Horses, introduced by Herr Nimsi.
14. The World-Famed Raynor Troupe.
15. Carlo Bianchi, the Barrel King.
16. Harry Austin, as the Newmarket Jockey.
17. The Flying Stellios.
18. The Wonderful Fire-Horse, "Kohinoor."

"GOD SAVE THE QUEEN."

Roll up! Roll up! The big top comes to Balmoral.

exceed the Queen's wonderful kindness to me, and I was quite overcome. She is such a wonderful woman animated & keen & talks away – she produced a large pair of glasses & said 'I must put on my glasses to have a good look at you'. I felt shy. When George came in for his audience she said I must congratulate you for your wife is both beautiful & wise![8]

Above, below and page 100: Three of the spectacular acts that made
Sanger's Circus the most famous of its day.

The Queen's final Spring holiday at Cimiez in 1899 provoked
intense friction. The Household were resolute and united: they
would force the Queen not to take Abdul Karim on the forth-
coming visit. Further messages from the Queen asking that
they should associate more with him, together with the style
he was accorded, had intensified their resolve.

To an increasingly frail and isolated old lady, it must have
given considerable pain to be harassed by the complaints of

those very people to whom she would ordinarily have looked for help. The prevailing tension within the Household must have exacerbated her notoriously bad nerves. She felt the force of their hostility, as many phrases in her letters to Sir James bear out: 'I thought you stood between me and them, but now I feel that you chime in with the rest.'[9]

Harriet Phipps was charged with the task of telling the Queen of her Household's ultimatum: either the Munshi should be left out of the suite accompanying her to the Riviera or they would all resign. Nothing could have prepared the Honourable Miss Phipps for the Queen's reaction. With one imperious gesture Her Majesty swept all the objects off her desk. Her Maid of Honour silently withdrew.

When the Queen duly set off with the Household, the Munshi was left behind, a victory for his enemies. No sooner had they arrived than fortunes were reversed. Having settled into the Excelsior Regina as usual, Her Majesty exerted her authority and simply sent for Abdul to follow on.

There were still interludes when the mood was more harmonious: while in the south that year, the Queen enjoyed an evening of music from *La Bohème* and *I Pagliacci*, played ('and beautifully', she said) by Leoncavallo.

Depite all the pressure brought by her Household, and even some of her Ministers over the years, the Queen remained steadfast and loyal to the Munshi. All close relationships have an element which defies explanation. Perhaps the nearest we can get to understanding this one is to remember the Queen's essentially lonely, isolated position, and her love of the exotic. In the absence of testimony from Abdul Karim, knowing him only through observations made by others, we cannot assess him as easily as the other characters in this story who have left us evidence.

All that can be said is that 'dear Abdul' had some quality of personality which made the Queen feel at home with him.

In the early evening of 22nd January 1901, Queen Victoria passed peacefully away at Osborne, her favourite home, planned so many years before with her beloved Albert. Despite his own aversion, her successor Edward VII recognised all that the Munshi had meant to his mother. Abdul Karim was therefore allowed to say his personal farewell. Led into her room, he saw the Queen's body covered by her bridal veil, surrounded by palms.

What were his thoughts as he saw the late Empress of India, who had been so motherly in her affection? Did he think of the eager pupil, so curious about his homeland and about the strange fate which had so improbably linked his life with hers? Abdul was allocated a place walking in the grand funeral procession, where he joined Kings and Princes.

Just as he had made the journey from total obscurity at the beginning, so at the end he had to return. It was a swift and painful severance, as the new King was eager for his departure. The Indian servants were also unceremoniously repatriated, but all were given a pension.

Just over six months after Queen Victoria's death, Lady Curzon recalled bygone days in a letter to her husband:

> Braemar Castle
> 9 August 1901
>
> ... Charlotte Knollys told me that the Munshi bogie which had frightened all the household at Windsor for many years had proved a ridiculous farce, as the poor man had not only given up *all* his letters but even the photos signed by Queen, and had returned to India like a whipped hound. All the Indian servants have gone back so that now there is no Oriental picture & queerness at Court. Lord Cromer told me (he *said* confidentially) that when Lord Rosebery offered him India he urged him to make up his mind quickly as it was of grave importance that the appointment should be made *before the Munshi* returned from India to England (he was on his way) as he might object & prevent any appointment! How funny this sounds now. Lord C. went on to say that all the Queen's Eastern ideas were the Munshi's and were invariably wrong – he had no opinion of her judgement which surprised me.[10]

Perhaps Rosebery had indulged in jocular exaggeration, but some significance can be attached to what people widely *believe* is happening, even if that belief does not express the whole truth.

Three of Queen Victoria's great-grandchildren with her Indian servant Abdullah: Prince Edward, Prince Albert and Princess Victoria of York. Balmoral 1898.

Four years later, on a tour of India, the Prince of Wales, later George V, penned the following letter to his father:

> Circuit House, Agra.
> 17th December 1905
>
> ... In the evening we saw the Munshi. He has not grown more beautiful and is getting fat. I must say he was most civil and humble and really pleased to see us. He wore his C.V.O. which I had no idea he had got. I am told he lives

quietly here and gives no trouble at all. We also saw dear Grandmamma's last four Indian servants who were with her up to her death; they also live here ....[11]

Postscript

The Munshi lived in comfortable retirement till his death in 1909.

Rafiuddin Ahmed, familiarly known as 'the Moulvi', returned to India and was elected to the Bombay Council in 1909. By virtue of the Montagu-Chelmsford reforms he became a Minister of the Bombay Government in 1928, his portfolio including Education. Knighted in 1932, Sir Rafiuddin spent the last twenty years of his life in Poona, where he loved to entertain visitors with tales of his youth at Queen Victoria's Court. He died in 1954.

Notes

Abbreviations
RA = The Royal Archives, Windsor Castle.
Vic. Add. = Victorian additional manuscripts under above reference.
IOR = India Office Records
MR = Reid Private Papers: published and unpublished material.
QVJ = Queen Victoria's Journal

1. Arrival

1. IOR D558/1 46, 28th November 1890.
2. RA QVJ, 21st June 1887.
3. RA QVJ, 3rd August 1887.
4. Major-Gen Thomas Dennehey, formerly Political Agent in Rajputana, who had been made Extra Groom in Waiting.
5. RA QVJ, 23rd June 1887.
6. RA A12/1504.
7. MR, QV to Dr Reid.
8. RA, L20/124.
9. *Morning Post* 27th April 1889.
10. *Ask Sir James* by Michaela Reid (Hodder and Stoughton 1987).
11. Ibid.
12. Ibid.
13. Ibid.

2. A Man of Property

1. IOR Eur. D558/1 no 28.
2. IOR Eur. D558/1 no 29.
3. IOR Eur. D558/1 no 36 & no 39.
4. IOR Eur. D558/1 no 38.
5. IOR Eur. D558/1 no 39.
6. *London Figaro*, 30th October 1890.
7. IOR Eur. D558/1 no 45.
8. IOR Eur. D558/1 no 46.
9. IOR Eur. D558/1 no 45.
10. IOR Eur. D558/1 no 57.

3. Enter Rafiuddin Ahmed

1. *Strand Magazine*, 2nd December 1892.
2. Ibid.
3. Ibid.
4. Later George V.
5. IOR Eur. F84/126a.

4. Domesticity and Italian Diversions

1. RA QVJ, 18th November 1893.
2. *Victoria: Biography of a Queen*, by Stanley Wientraub (Unwin Hyman 1987).
3. *Letters from Queen Victoria to the Empress Frederick, 1886-1901*, edited by Agatha Ramm (Alan Sutton 1990).
4. RA Add. U104/10.
5. RA Add. U104/12.
6. *Standard*, 17th March 1894.
7. *Truth*, 15th February and 8th March 1894.
8. *Westminster Gazette*, 6th April 1894.
9. RA Add. A12/2/146.
10. *Ask Sir James*, op. cit. in ch. 1, n. 10.

5. The Fatal Christmas Card

1. IOR Eur. F84/126b, 16th January 1895, F. Ponsonby to Lord Elgin.
2. IOR Eur. F84/126b, 25th January 1895, F. Ponsonby to Lord Elgin.
3. IOR Eur. F84/126b, 13th February 1895, A. Durand to F. Ponsonby.
4. IOR Eur. F84/126b, 15th February 1895, Lord Elgin to Mr Fowler.
5. RA Add. U104/17, Queen Victoria to Abdul Karim.
6. MR, Reid Diary.
7. RA H37/46, October 1895, Queen Victoria to Lord Salisbury.

6. The Munshi Triumphant

1. *Lady Lytton's Court Diary*, edited by Lady Mary Lutyens (Rupert Hart-Davis 1961).
2. Ibid.
3. IOR Eur. A147/4, Queen Victoria to Lord George Hamilton.
4. *Letters from Queen Victoria to the Empress Frederick*, op. cit.
5. *Truth*, 19th December 1895.
6. IOR Eur. F84/126a, Lord George Hamilton to Lord Elgin.
7. IOR Eur. F84/126b, Lord Elgin to Lord Sandhurst.

7. A Year of Battles

1. IOR Eur. F84/126a, 27th April 1897, Fritz Ponsonby to H. Babbington-Smith.
2. MR, Reid Diary, 4th April 1897.
3. Ibid, 5th April 1897.
4. *Galignani Messenger*, Nice.

5. IOR C/25/2 169, 30th April 1897, private correspondence between Lord G. Hamilton and Lord Elgin 1895-1898.
6. IOR D509 Vol V, 18th May 1897, Elgin to Lord George Hamilton.
7. IOR C/25/2/97, 14th May 1897, Lord George Hamilton to Elgin.
8. MR, Queen Victoria to Dr Reid
9. Ibid.
10. MR, Reid Diary, 1897.
11. Ibid.
12. Ibid.
13. Salisbury Papers, Queen Victoria to Lord Salisbury, 31st July 1897.
14. Salisbury Papers, Queen Victoria to Lord Salisbury 17th September 1897.
15. Salisbury Papers, Queen Victoria to Lord Salisbury 17th July 1897.

8. The Chill Winds of Autumn

1. MR, Queen Victoria to Dr Reid.
2. MR, Reid Diary.
3. MR, Queen Victoria to Dr Reid.
4. Ibid.
5. Ibid.
6. *World*, 15th September 1897
7. MR, Reid Diary.

9. A Prince Manqué

1. *The Times*, 13th January 1898.
2. Reid Corr. Reid PP.
3. Salisbury Papers, Queen Victoria to Lord Salisbury, 6th June 1898.
4. RA U/104/20.
5. MR, Reid Diary & Correspondence.
6. Ibid.
7. Ibid.
8. *Lady Curzon's India: Letters from a Vicereine*, edited by John Bradley (Weidenfeld and Nicolson 1985).
9. MR, Reid Correspondence.
10. *Lady Curzon's India*, op. cit.
11. RA GV AA27/10.

Index

AK = Abdul Karim; QV = Queen Victoria; page numbers in italics refer to illustrations.

Abdullah, *103*
Adeane, Marie, *55*, 76
Agra, 14, 15, 24, 26, 27, 74, 92, 103
Ahmed, Rafiuddin, 35-41, *38*, 49, 61, 77, 79, 80, 81,
    86, 94, 95, 96, 105
  suspected agent of Amir of Afghanistan, 36
  writes for *Strand Magazine*, 36-9
  and Muslim Patriotic League, 93
Albany, Duchess of, 28-9, 30
Alberta, Royal Yacht, 67
Ali, Hourmet (AK's brother-in-law), 20
Ali, Khairat, *70*
Alix of Hesse, Princess, *17, 70*
Arthur Cottage, Osborne, *68*

Babbington-Smith, Sir Henry, 55, 76
Ballater, 28-9, 90
Balmoral Castle, 16, 19-21, 26, 27, *28*, 89
  Garden Cottage, *20*, 64
  visit of Queen of Roumania, 27-30
  tableau vivant at, *31*
Battersea, Lady, 76
Bayley, Charles A., 41, 81
Beatrice, Princess, *25*, 28, 29, 30, 70, 76
Bigge, Sir Arthur, *47*, 54, 55, 61, 80, *85*
Black and White, 35, 60
Bombay, 29
Borghese, Pauline, 48
Bradford, Sir Ernest, 36, 94, 96
Breadalbane, Lord, 77
Brown, John, 21, 54
Bukhsh, Mohammed, 15, *16, 17, 25, 31, 70*

Campbell, Mrs, *31*
Cecil, Lady Edward, 58
Chidda, Sheikh, *46, 71*
Churchill, Lady, *47*, 48, *85*

Cimiez, 97
  QV stays at Hotel Excelsior Regina, 75-7, 80, 101
  Battle of Flowers, 76
  QV's final holiday there, 100-1
Clarence, Duke of, 28, 29
Cochrane, Minnie, *31*
Connaught, Duke of, *17*
Cowell, Sir John, *47*
Cross, Lord, 55
Curzon, Lady, 97, 102
Curzon, Lord, Viceroy of India, 97-8

Davidson, Sir Arthur, 77, *85*
Deccan College, Poona, 35
Durand, A., 55

Edward VII, 101
Edwards, Sir Fleetwood, 54, *55*, 80, 83
Elgin, 9th Earl of, Viceroy of India, 53-8, *57*, 69-73,
  72, 80
Elgin, Lady, 54, 56

Florence Gazette, 50
Frederick of Germany, Empress, 45, 67
Frogmore Cottage, 43, 92

Galignani Messenger, 79
George V, 103
Glassalt Shiel, QV's private retreat on Loch
  Muick, 21
Graphic, 89-90
Grasse
  Grand Hotel, *75*
  Alice de Rothschild's 'Villa Victoria', 76

Hamilton, Lord George, Secretary of State for
  India, 65, 69-73, 80, 82

Harris, Lord, 55
Henry of Battenberg, Prince, *17*, 28, 30, 48, *59*
Henry of Battenberg, Princess, 17, 48, *59*
Hussain, Abdul, *70*
Hussain, Ahmed, 84

Indian servants, 54, *59*, 104
    arrival of in Royal Household, 13
    uniform for Balmoral, 16
    repatriated after QV's death, 102
Irene of Hesse, Princess, *17*
Irving, Henry, in command performance of *The Bells* at Sandringham, 18-19

Jenner, Sir William, 21
Jowett, Dr, 40

Karim, Abdul, *12*, *17*, *25*, *31*, *44*, *51*, *64*, *70*, *91*
    arrival in Royal Household, 13-14
    first meeting with QV, 14
    Munshi ('Teacher') and QV's Indian Secretary, 14, 67-8
    Order of Eastern Star, 14, 43
    teaches QV Hindustani, 17, 22, 92
    helps QV with correspondence, 17-18
    accompanies QV to Glassalt Shiel, 21
    becomes ill, 21-2
    grant of land by QV, 23-7, 32-3
    visit to India in 1890, 32-3
    and Rafiuddin Ahmed, 35-41
    wife, 43-8, 63-4, 69
    accompanies QV to Florence, 48
    sends Christmas card to Lord Elgin, 54-8
    created C.I.E., 58, *60*
    QV's adviser on Indian affairs, 65-6
    under surveillance in India in 1896, 69-74
    orders photograph published in *Graphic*, 89-90
    returns to India after QV's death, 102
    created C.V.O., 103
    dies, 105
King's College, London, 35

Lansdowne, Lady, 26-7, 33
Lansdowne, Lord, Viceroy of India, 11, *24*
    and grant of land to AK, 23-6, 32-3
    receives AK in India, 32
Lee-Warner, Sir William, 81
Louis of Battenberg, Prince, 77-8
Louise of Wales, Princess, *70*
Lytton, Lady, 63-5, *85*
    Court Diary, 63-5
    describes AK's wife, 63-4
Marie of Edinburgh, Princess, *17*

Mary of Teck, Princess, *40*
Menton, Fête des Citrons, 76
Middle Temple, 35
Moore, Miss, *31*
Morning Post, 19
Munshi, *see* Abdul Karim
Muslim League, 35, 93
Muslim Patriotic league, 93
Mustapha, *71*

Nairoji, Dadabhai, 35, 93
Nineteenth Century, 86

Osborne House, *74*
    alfresco tea at, *17*
    Durbar Hall, 15
    theatricals at, *25*
Ouseley, Gore, 49

Pall Mall Gazette, 35
Phipps, Hon. Harriet, 48, 55, 58, 63, *85*, 101
Ponsonby, Frederick ('Fritz'), 53-6, *55*, 76-7
Ponsonby, Sir Henry, QV's Private Secretary, 17, 18, *25*, *47*, 50, 53, *66*, 67

Raschid, Abdul, *91*
Reid, Dr (later Sir) James, Queen's Physician, 18, 19, 21, *22*, 45, *47*, 48, 50, 54, *55*, 58, 78, 83-4, *85*, 90, 92, 94, 96
Rosebery, Lord, 102
Rothschild, Alice de 76
Roumania, Queen of, visits Balmoral, 27-30
Royal Household, *85*
    animosity towards AK, 18, 19, 48, 75-87, 89-92, 97
    threaten to resign, 77-8, 101

Salisbury, 3rd Marquess of, 39, 58, 61, 83, 86, 87, 94, *95*, 96
Sandhurst, Lord, 73
Sandringham House, 19
Sanger, 'Lord' George, 97-100
    Sanger's Circus, *98*, *99*, *100*
Scheffer, Mr, Queen of Roumania's private secretary, 27-30
Strand Magazine, 35
Swoboda, Rudolph, 15, 38, 39-40
Sylva, Carmen, *see* Roumania, Queen of

Terry, Ellen, command performance of *The Bells* at Sandringham, 18-19
Times, The, 93
Tuck, Mrs, QV's dresser, 20
Turkey, Sultan of, 39, 40

Tuxen, Laurits R., *40*
Tyler, Sir John, Governor of N.W. Provinces, 13,
   32-3, 58

Viceregal Lodge, Simla, *24*, 25
Victoria Eugenie of Battenberg, Princess, *14*
Victoria Melita of Edinburgh, Princess, *17*
Victoria, Queen, *17*, *46*, *59*, *64*, *71*
   proclaimed Empress of India, 11
   Golden Jubilee, 11, 13
   Journal, 11-12, 14
   Hindustani Diary, *13*, 35, 36, 39
   learns Hindustani, 14, 22
   arranges grant of land in India to AK, 23-7, 32-3
   interest in AK's wife, 43-8
   decorates AK with Order of Eastern Star, 43
   holiday in Florence, 48, 50
   creates AK C.I.E., 58

   and Rafiuddin Ahmed, 61
   on holiday in Cimiez, 75-6, 101
   wishes to create AK K.C.I.E. and C.V.O., 82-3
   Diamond Jubilee, 84
   dies, 101
Villa Fabbricotti, 48
Von Angeli,. *51*

Wales, Prince of, 28; *see also* Edward VII
Wales, Princess of, 30
Wenlock, Lord, 55
Westminster Gazette, 49
Windsor Castle, 15, 58, *59*
World, 91-2

York, Duke of, 39, *40*
Yorke, Hon Alexander, *47*, *55*